# Healthy Indian Curry Dishes

EASY, HEALTHY DISHES THE WHOLE FAMILY WILL LOVE

**Hari Ghotra**

FAIR WINDS

**Quarto.com**



First Published in 2023 by Fair Winds Press, an imprint of The Quarto Group,
100 Cummings Center, Suite 265-D, Beverly, MA 01915, USA.
T (978) 282-9590 F (978) 283-2742



28 27 26 25 24 1 2 3 4 5

ISBN: 978-0-7603-9333-8

Digital edition published in 2023
eISBN: 978-0-7603-7718-5

The content in this book was previously published as *Indian for Everyone* by Hari Ghotra (Fair Winds Press 2023).

Library of Congress Cataloging-in-Publication Data is available under *Indian for Everyone*.

Design and page layout: Laura Shaw Design
Cover illustrations by Shutterstock.
Photography: Mark Deeprose, Thomas Alexander, and Shutterstock on pages 11, 7, and 49

Printed in China

# Contents

# Introduction

**WHEN MY EDITOR** first suggested the title of this book, I thought it was a bit obvious—*of course* Indian food is for everyone! But if you've never had much exposure to spice, or if you're worried it will be complex and time-consuming to cook Indian food, I'm here to set the record straight. Indian food is actually not that complicated, and the flavors and techniques can add new dimensions to standard British or American fare, at any meal (even breakfast). So maybe you're a mom or dad looking for a quick, healthy weeknight dinner or planning an elaborate family feast. Maybe you like the idea of using spices, but you're a little unsure about where to start. Or maybe you are looking for fun ideas for a glam dinner party with your friends, a fresh and fiery barbecue, or a tasty vegetarian (or vegan) spread. It could even be that you are feeling a little under the weather and need a warming, spicy pick-me-up to give you a hug from the inside out.

Whatever the case, these are some of my favorite recipes, which illustrate how you can make Indian flavors part of your everyday life (and special occasions, of course!). The recipes in this book are unique in that they blend the influence of my family and ancestors with the tricks I have picked up. I hope your confidence increases and you'll feel inspired to make these dishes on your own.

## IT ALL STARTS WITH A LITTLE SPICE

If you've never cooked with spices, I hope this book gives you the confidence to start. Understanding what they do and how to use them will forever change the way you view food.

Spices are not just about flavor and aromatics; in Indian cooking their contributions are much more holistic: They can be used to delicately soothe and aid digestion, induce an internal cooling or warming sensation, stimulate the immune system, and so much more—the delicious taste they infuse doesn't hurt either. Once you pluck up the courage to get started, I've even given you some red-hot tips on how to crank up the punchiness for those who love a kick, and how to mellow things down for those with a more delicate palate. I have also tried to show you how you can adjust the dishes for people with differing dietary requirements.

If you are a novice when cooking Indian food or an old hand, there is always something new to try. Indian food continues to evolve as new influences, new ideas, and new cooking techniques come to the scene.

As a British-born Indian, I have seen how Indian food has been adopted into everyday life in the U.K. As a nation we love Indian cuisine; the United Kingdom is probably the most advanced Western country in its journey and love affair with the cuisine. Being lucky enough to travel the world with my job, I have realized that the flavors I am used to at home are now impacting all parts of the world in so many different cuisines. They are now familiar to so many people, and having a curry or an Indian meal (as exciting as it is) is becoming part of their everyday repertoire.

### TIPS FOR COOKING AN INDIAN CURRY

When preparing any dish, I first think about what I am hoping to end up with because then I know what I need to do during the cooking process to achieve that outcome. Am I looking for a deep, dark, moody meat curry or a light, fragrant fish curry or a dry vegetable side dish? Once you have the answer, you will be able to define the ingredients you need, how to prepare them, and how to cook the dish to achieve the desired goal.

"It's all about the onions!" Many (though not all) Indian dishes start with onions, to make a basic masala. Before we cook our onions, it's important to get them chopped to the right shape and size for your dish—are you looking for a smooth, creamy sauce or a chunky one? This will define whether you slice, chop, grate, or blitz your onions.

How you brown your onions can also make or break your dish. When I teach my cooking classes, I tell my students that Indian food is all about how you treat your onions. A deep, dark curry requires the onions to be cooked down until they are soft and dark, which gives you not only the color you are looking for but also the depth of flavor. There are two main ways to effectively brown your onions: a low, slow cook during which the onion cells break down to make a paste; or at a higher temperature during which the onions brown more quickly, resulting in browned onions that still have texture and shape.

Technically when we cook our onions like this, we are not caramelizing them because they don't contain enough sugar to reach the temperatures required for caramelization. We are browning them through the Maillard process during which there's a reaction between the sugars, carbohydrates, amino acids, and heat, resulting in a complex meaty flavor as the onions cook.

Choose onions that are pungent—brown/yellow or white—as these will brown better because they have higher sulfur compounds than a less pungent onion, such as a red onion.

- For a deep, dark, slow-cooked meat dish, gently cook your onions to a dark brown color until the onion starts to break down. Start on a high heat to disperse the moisture. Reduce the heat and stir the onions until a dark brown color is achieved, adding a splash of water every time the onions stick to the pan.
- For a light vegetable or lentil dish in which you want the vegetables to sing, the onions need to be cooked only until they are a wonderfully golden brown color.
- For a white masala or a fish dish that's light and fresh, the onions are cooked only until translucent or just starting to color.

## MAKING INDIAN FOR EVERYONE

Here are a few easy tips you can use to ensure the Indian meals you cook are suitable for everyone in the family, whatever their age, dietary requirement, likes, or dislikes.

### *Children*

Get them eating spices early—I weaned my kids on Kitcheree, which is a delicate lentil and rice porridge that's easy to digest but still flavorful.

For young kids, dial down the salt, chillies, and garlic.

Most kids love breads, so naans, rotis, and parathas are a great way to get them dipping into sauces and chutneys.

Kids love food they can pick up, so finger foods like kebabs and pakora are great.

If you involve your children in the cooking of a dish, they will be more likely to try it.

It doesn't have to be hot to be tasty. So if you are cooking for children (or someone who doesn't like hot food), remove or tone down the number of chillies you use during cooking, or separate out portions without chillies.

I find children are often put off by different textures. My kids used to dislike chunks of onions, so I would make the masala and then purée their portion.

Add a little creaminess and sweetness with yogurt, cream, or coconut milk. If anyone has a problem with lactose, instead soak almonds or cashews in boiling water until they soften, and then blend to a purée before adding to the dish.

### *Vegetarians*

Indian food is a great option for vegetarians because the masalas and spice add a depth of flavor that works well with many different vegetables.

Dhal, beans, and legumes are great with spices, and they are a fantastic source of protein. But be sure you know exactly what you are using so you cook it long enough.

In most of my recipes, you can replace the meat with vegetables. If it's a long, slow-cooked dish, choose vegetables that will hold up to a longer cooking time, even though you will still need to reduce the cooking time.

There are lots of unique Indian vegetables that I would urge you to try, from okra to snake beans, karela to tindora—just do a little research on the best way to prepare them.

### *Vegan or Plant-Based Diets*

The Indian diet is superb if you are vegan because it uses a vast array of beans, lentils, and legumes as well as vegetables.

Many masalas are vegan already, so they require very little manipulation.

Milk-based elements are common in Indian cuisine—namely ghee, yogurts, and raita. But most dishes work just fine with standard milk substitutes. Here are my suggestions:

- Replace ghee/butter with coconut oil.
- To make raita or dips, replace yogurt with the many dairy-free alternatives that are now available.
- To replace cream, use coconut cream/milk or a cornstarch slurry made with a nondairy milk and a touch of maple syrup.
- To thicken sauces, use nut pastes made by soaking nuts and blending them with a nondairy milk.
- Paneer can be replaced with soya protein, tempeh, or tofu.
- Get familiar with aquafaba, or bean water (the water from a tin of chickpeas); it whips up like egg whites and can be used to make mayonnaise and even meringues.

### *Gluten Free*

Most Indian dishes are naturally gluten free. Spices, basic masalas, and sauces are already free from ingredients containing gluten. Sauces are not usually thickened using wheat flours either.

Indian breads like roti, poori, and naan are naturally the most challenging for a gluten-free diner, as they are made with wheat flour. There are many wheat-free flours you can try. I have experimented with different brands to varying success, but the results are different as they come out more like flatbreads rather than the puffy breads we are used to. Alternative options include:

- breads/pancakes made using gram flour—chilla, pudla
- crepes made using lentil or rice batters—dosa, idli
- breads made using fermented rice batters—idli, appam

### *Allium Intolerance*

More common than you think, allium intolerance causes the body to launch an immune response resulting in severe digestive problems. This intolerance can be triggered when onions, garlic, spring onions, leeks, or chives are consumed. The only way to manage it is through avoiding these items in your diet. You may think that this means Indian food is out, but that's not true. There is a segment of the Hindu religion who are known as Jains. They believe in total nonviolence, which includes what they eat—no meat and no plants that are extracted from the ground (potatoes, onions, garlic, and so on) as they would be able to continue growing. They consume only berries, legumes, and fruits that do not harm the plant when picked. There are a number of things you can do to ensure you have a nice, flavorful meal without garlic or onions.

Asafoetida is the dried, powdered resin that comes from the sap of a giant fennel-like plant that grows in Iran. It has a bitter, acrid flavor and smells really awful when raw, but once fried it gives a wonderful aroma and the flavor profile of onions and garlic to your dish. It should be used only in tiny amounts as it is very pungent. You treat it as a whole spice and add it to hot oil at the start of the cooking process. It's used in lentil and vegetable dishes to give the pungency of onions when they are not present in the recipe. Used a lot in Kashmiri, Maharashtrian, and South Indian cooking, it is known to have many health benefits, including its anti-flatulence properties and its ability to soothe digestive problems.

If you have an intolerance to onions, other options that give you the texture and body of an onion include fennel, carrots, celery, and even parsnips. If you don't like onions and need something milder, then shallots or spring onions are also an option.

Here is an example of how you use asafoetida in a traditional curry.

# Lamb Rogan Josh

**Serves 4-6**

2 tablespoons (30 ml) mustard oil
large pinch asafoetida
1 teaspoon cumin seeds
1 stick of cassia bark
3 cloves
2 whole dried Kashmiri chillies
2 black cardamom pods
2 green cardamom pods
1 teaspoon salt
2 pounds (800 g) leg of lamb, cut into large chunks
1 teaspoon red Kashmiri chilli powder (or ratanjot, if you have it)
1 teaspoon hot chilli powder (optional)
1 teaspoon ginger powder
1 teaspoon fennel powder
3 heaped tablespoons (45 g) Greek yogurt
3 to 4 tablespoons (50 ml) water
1 teaspoon garam masala

In a wide pan, heat the mustard oil on high heat to smoking point before removing from the heat. Allow it to cool; then reheat on low heat and add the asafoetida. Once it sizzles, add all the whole spices—cumin seeds, cassia, cloves, dried chillies, black and green cardamoms—and salt to taste.

Once the spices become fragrant, add the meat and fry until it turns a lovely brown color. Reduce the heat, add the chilli powders (or ratanjot, if you have it), and let the meat cook for a few minutes (leave on a low heat so the chilli powder doesn't burn).

Add the ginger and fennel powders.

Stir in the yogurt 1 tablespoon at a time. Once mixed through, place the lid on the pan and leave on the lowest heat setting to gently simmer for up to an hour. Check after 30 minutes and add some water if needed, leaving to cook until the meat is tender.

Once the meat is tender, add enough boiling water to cover the meat to create a lovely gravy. Allow it to simmer gently for 5–7 minutes, and then add the garam masala and serve.

***Nightshade Intolerance***

I often get asked about nightshade intolerance in my line of work, usually referring to tomatoes. The likelihood is that if you are intolerant to tomatoes, you will have an intolerance to potatoes, eggplants, and even latex. This intolerance is known to cause digestive issues but also other issues ranging from joint pain, stiffness, headaches, nausea, and even skin irritations. To avoid tomatoes in your diet, you can select curries without tomatoes such as Korma, dry vegetable dishes, and rogan josh. You can substitute the tomatoes for yogurt to add tartness and a silky mouth feel.

If you just don't like tomatoes, another option is to roast or blacken red peppers , and then blitz them to a paste to add depth. Many dishes that traditionally include tomatoes can also be cooked successfully without them.

## ALL ABOUT SPICES

We talk about spices all the time, but do you actually know what they are? Spices are vegetative substances—a fruit, a seed, bark, or even skin—that are used in small quantities as food additives to enhance (or hide!) flavors, to add color, or to preserve. These little gems also have many other properties that can be used in medicine, cosmetics, and perfumery. For example, cloves contain a chemical called eugenol that inhibits the growth of bacteria, and the active agent in turmeric is curcumin, which is responsible not only for its bright yellow color but for its effectiveness as an anti-inflammatory.

As a result, many spices are routinely used in various forms of alternative medicine.

### PROPERTIES OF SPICES

Different spices have warming or cooling effects on our bodies. Just as Mother Earth gives us specific plants at certain times of the year so our bodies can get the nutrients they need, so are spices used seasonally in Indian cooking. For example, dishes that contain mustard seeds are prepared when the season is changing and we are more prone to colds, because mustard seeds contain minerals that help to ward off these bugs.

Spices come in either a whole form (in their natural state) or ground to a powder. It is always best to go with whole spices and grind them yourself when you need them, if possible. This way they will retain their natural oils for longer, and therefore retain their flavor-enhancing properties.

### USING SPICES

The way you use spices matters. Depending on whether they are roasted, ground, boiled, or crushed, they will give a slightly different aromatic. With spices, less is more, and small amounts can have a huge impact on the dish you are cooking. If you are a novice, start with something gentle like cumin, and as you experiment more, you will discover which flavors you like.

To determine how and when spices should be added, I categorize them into groups based on when they are added to the pan. This should give you a framework to use spices more effectively and also allow your dishes to have that delicate layering of flavor that curries are known for.

#### *Stage 1: Base—Whole Spices*

These are generally tempered, which means they are heated in hot oil (or dry fried) at the beginning of the cooking process to release their natural oils gradually. Whole spices include cassia bark, green cardamom, cloves, cumin seeds, mustard seeds, and bay leaves. They form the base flavor of your dish and are added at the beginning. Not every dish requires whole spices, especially simple ones.

#### *Stage 2: Vibrancy—Taste and Color Spices*

These are added to the pan one at a time, usually midway through the recipe. They typically come in powder form, meaning the oils are released more readily, so you don't want to add them at the start, as the aromatics will dissipate too quickly. They should also be added to a liquid base, to prevent them from burning. So once the tomatoes, yogurt, or coconut milk has gone in, the ground spices go in. This group includes chilli, coriander, cumin, and turmeric.

#### *Stage 3: Finesse—Delicate Aromatic Spices*

These are the more delicate spices such as cardamom, mace, or garam masala—powders that are added at the end of the cooking process. These enhance the final flavor profiles and add the final aromas of the dish. Delicate herbs, like fresh coriander and dried fenugreek (methi), will also go in at the end.

### STORING SPICES

Spices are natural ingredients, and the purpose of using them is to harness their natural oils. So it's important that we keep those vital oils inside as long as possible. Generally, whole spices, if stored correctly, will keep fresh for nine to twelve months. Ground spices, if stored correctly, will keep for six to nine months.

Here is my advice:

- Store spices in airtight containers in a dark space, not near a heat source.
- Invest in an Indian masala dabba, which is a spice box that is dark and airtight; plus it keeps all your spices in one place.
- Buy spices whole and grind them when required.
- Taste and smell your spices to judge if they are fresh.

### TEN KEY SPICES

***Cumin Seeds (Jeera)***

These brown oval seeds can be used whole or ground and will give a warming pungent flavor. Beautifully aromatic, cumin brings out the natural sweetness of a dish. When used whole, they add a nutty flavor and texture. I always buy cumin whole and crush it as needed.

***Coriander Seeds (Dhania)***

These round, beige seeds are warming and fragrant when crushed. The seeds release a gentle citrus flavor almost like lemon or orange. They are known to help reduce cholesterol and have a cooling effect on the body. If you suffer from nasal congestion, you could boil a teaspoon of coriander seeds in a mug of water, strain, cool, and drink to help relieve the tension.

Planting these seeds will result in a beautiful coriander plant with very delicate, highly perfumed flat leaves that give off a light freshness. The flavor is completely different from that of the coriander seeds, so do not substitute one for the other.

***Turmeric (Haldi)***

Related to ginger, turmeric is a root that is dried and ground to create a bright yellow powder (the iconic "curry" color). It has a chalky texture and a woody aroma with slightly bitter undertones.

***Chillies (Mirch)***

The many varieties can be used fresh or sun-dried, whole or ground to a powder. Fresh green finger chillies are the chilli of choice to add heat and freshness. My preferred variety of chilli powder is Kashmiri, as it's mild and gives a gentle, smoked warmth, plus a beautifully vibrant red color. All chilli powders are different—some can be smoky and others much more fiery—so it's a good idea to know what you are using.

***Dried Fenugreek Leaves (Kasoori Methi)***

The herb and the seed are two very different ingredients, and it's not a great idea to substitute the spice for the herb. The green powder, or dried green herb, is made from the leaves of the plant. Used to flavor lamb and lentil dishes, it has a very characteristic, musky "curry" aroma with a slight bitter taste. Young fresh leaves are used as greens, more like spinach. Fenugreek seeds are beige in color and look like little stones. They can be ground down to a powder and have a very strong, bitter, earthy flavor. Using too much of the ground seeds when cooking can be very overpowering; you only need half a teaspoon for a meal serving eight people.

***Garam Masala***

Literally, "garam" means warm, and "masala" is a spice blend. An aromatic blend of spices, it usually contains cumin, black pepper, coriander seeds, cassia bark, carom seeds, black cardamom, cloves, green cardamom, and bay leaves, which leaves a delicate warming sensation. Indian families often have their own special blend of garam masala, and so do I. Garam masala is probably one of the most important ingredients in northern Indian food, usually added at the end of the cooking process to intensify and refresh all the flavors and fragrances of the dish.

***Mustard Seeds (Sarson)***

These come in three varieties—white, brown, or black. When these tiny round seeds are heated, they release a unique nose-tingling pungency, like that of horseradish. Indian cooking generally uses black or brown seeds. It's a harsh spice great for pickles and achaar in vegetable and lentil dishes. A great combination for Indian vegetable dishes is cumin and mustard; together, they offer both warmth and bite. High in magnesium, mustard seeds are known to assist in lowering blood pressure and aiding digestion.

### *Cassia Bark (Dal Chini) and Cinnamon*

Cassia bark is related to cinnamon, but it isn't the same. Cassia adds a sweeter, milder flavor, whereas cinnamon has a stronger, harsher, hotter flavor. Cassia originated in Southeast Asia from one tree variety called *Cinnamomum*, which is known as Chinese or true cinnamon. It is thicker, like the outer bark of a tree, and darker in color. Most other cinnamon comes from related species that are generally referred to as cassia.

Cinnamon is lighter beige in color and made up of wafer-thin quills. Most of the world's cinnamon quills are produced in Sri Lanka. Cassia is usually cheaper than cinnamon as very little labor is required to produce it, whereas cinnamon quills require a workforce. For all my Indian dishes, I use cassia rather than cinnamon.

Both are used in desserts as well as savory and rice dishes. In those lighter, sweeter dishes such as a Korma or Pasanda, it gives the very subtle sweetness that these dishes are known for.

### *Cloves (Laung)*

These are dried flower pods that look like miniature black scepters. They have a very strong, distinct flavor that comes from the chemical eugenol, so they should be used sparingly. In any one dish you would only need three or four of them. Cloves leave a warming sensation and are generally used in dishes both sweet and savory alongside their sister spice, green cardamom.

### *Green Cardamom (Elachi)*

These are small green pods, each containing about twenty black seeds. They are commonly used in traditional Indian sweets, desserts, Indian chai, and savory meat dishes. Green cardamom is also an important ingredient in some spice blends. The pods themselves are quite fibrous, but they can be ground down to a powder or used whole, or you can remove the husk and pound the seeds. They have a bittersweet flavor and an intense aromatic perfume that people usually either love or hate. You would only use three or four pods at a time, and they should be stored whole, because once the seeds are exposed, they lose their aromatics very quickly. Ensure your cardamom pods are green when you use them, as it's the green color that indicates they have the desired aromatics in them.

**A NOTE ABOUT CURRY POWDER:**

This is an all-in-one spice blend that gives a very generic curry taste. It's not used by Indian cooks to make curry because they would always use the individual spices specific to the dish being cooked. There is no real recipe to make it, but a mild one generally includes cumin, coriander, and turmeric; a hot curry powder may include chilli powder; and a madras includes black pepper, mustard, and ginger. Other commercial blends may also include clove, cardamom, bay leaf, and fenugreek.

## CLASSIC INDIAN COOKING TECHNIQUES

There are a number of classic Indian cooking techniques used in authentic Indian stovetop cooking. Used differently for various dishes, they all play a part in infusing a dish with flavor and aromatics.

### *Tadka (Tempering)*

Tadka, baghar, and chowkna are all the same principle but called different things in different regions. Known in English as tempering, this method is about infusing whole spices in hot oil or ghee to intensify their natural flavors and to create a fragrant oil that is used either at the beginning of the cooking process, for the base flavor of the dish, or as the final garnish, as with some dhals and chutneys.

### ***Bhuna or Bhuno (Stir-Fry to Reduce)***

This method is a mixture of stir-frying and sautéing: sautéing and browning (usually onions) over a low-and-slow heat at the start of the cooking process, creating real depth and intensity for the base masala, then letting the onions just melt away into the sauce. You can also bhun meat dishes at the end of the cooking time over a high heat; this intensifies the flavor and reduces the sauce until it clings to the meat.

### ***Dhum or Dum (Steam Infusion)***

This method is essentially steaming or simmering on very low heat over a long cooking period in a vessel that is sealed closed. The process allows the ingredients to cook in their own juices and, if cooking meat on the bone, the marrow renders out to pack the dish full of flavor. The results of this method are very close to those achieved by a slow cooker.

This is the traditional technique (two hundred years old) of cooking a biryani known as dum pukht, where rice and spiced meat are layered in a round-bottomed clay or metal vessel called a handi. By trapping the steam inside, it allowed the fragrance of the spices to infuse into the rice and cook very slowly over a low heat or low burning embers. The dough, known as purdah or veil, was used to seal the pot. Sometimes, a hot coal was placed on the top, which essentially created an oven so it cooked from the top down and the bottom up. Once the dish was cooked, the chef would tap the vessel and if it made a "dum" sound, the dish was ready. The seal would be opened, allowing the spices and aromatics to float out and invite all to come to dinner.

### ***Talna (Frying)***

This is the process of cooking food by immersing it in hot oil—both deep and shallow frying. Key points to remember are that the oil needs to be between 349°F and 375°F (176°C to 190°C) to fry effectively. If it's too cold, the food will soak up the oil and become greasy; if it's too hot, it will burn on the outside and be raw in the center. I was always taught to check the temperature by dropping in a little of the ingredient or batter—if it sinks to the bottom and floats to the top straightaway, it is ready.

### ***Dhunaar (Smoke Seasoning)***

This is a more unusual process that involves a quick smoking process using burning charcoal in a closed pot to infuse a smoky flavor. It can be used for meat dishes, dhals, and so on. I use this with some chutneys to give them a smoked flavor. It's easy to do in your kitchen using a foil tray or a makeshift tinfoil tray. Heat coals over some flames on your cooker. Set the foil tray inside the pan you are wanting to smoke. Place the burning coals on the foil, add some whole spices, and pour over a tablespoon of ghee so it begins to smoke. Cover the pan and leave the smoke to infuse into the food for ten to fifteen minutes. It's a common method used in the desert areas of northern India, especially in the colder months.

### ***Tawa Cooking (Griddle)***

A tawa is a round, thin, concave cast-iron griddle pan. Helpful when very high temperatures are needed, it is mostly used in the home to cook unleavened breads, such as roti or paratha. On street corners in India, these huge griddles cook unique dishes that require fast cooking. The outside rim is used to keep the dishes warm as they are being sold. Snacks like pav bhaji and aloo tikki are typical tawa dishes. The veg masala is cooked in the center and constantly stirred to avoid burning. It's then smeared on bread rolls and sold. Other dishes include tawa chicken, tawa vegetables, and tawa paneer.

***Galavat***

Galavat refers to a method where softening agents like raw papaya paste (which contains papain), pineapple, mango, or yogurt are used to tenderize meat. In countries where the meat may be tougher or the type of meat requires more cooking (such as goat), these ingredients are very important. This method is slightly different from marinating because the process of marinating is more about penetrating the meat with other flavors, whereas this is solely about tenderizing. That said, you can also add other spices to infuse more flavor into the dish.

***Loab/Rogan***

Referring to the final stage of cooking, the oil used rises to the surface of the dish. It makes it look glossy and luxurious. This stage gives a dish that's been slowly cooked in a gravy its finished appearance.

# 1

# Feisty Finger Foods

Did you know that traditionally, Indian food is always consumed with your fingers? It has nothing to do with lack of cutlery or utensils—it's more about the holistic and spiritual approach Indians take to their food.

# Schmokin' Tandoori Wings

**Wings are the best type of finger food, because one wing is never enough! The zingy lime, fresh coriander, red chilli, and red onion slices sprinkled over the top add a tangy salad flavor, that complements that which has been imparted from the marinade.**

**Makes 12-15**

- 2¼ pounds (1 kg) chicken wings split into drumettes and flats
- ¾ cup (200 g) Greek yogurt
- 4 garlic cloves, crushed
- 2 teaspoons fresh ginger, grated
- juice from 1 lemon
- 1 tablespoon garam masala
- 2 teaspoons Kashmiri chilli powder
- 1 teaspoon cumin seeds, crushed
- 1 teaspoon salt
- 1 tablespoon dried fenugreek leaves (kasoori methi)
- 1 tablespoon gram flour
- 1 tablespoon (15 ml) mustard oil

**TO SERVE**

- fresh lime wedges
- fresh coriander, chopped
- red chillies, sliced (optional)
- red onion, sliced

Preheat the oven to 400°F (204°C, or gas mark 6).

Combine all the marinade ingredients together and stir.

Place the chicken wings in the bowl, and coat them fully with the marinade. Allow to marinate for at least 30 minutes (but you can leave them for up to 24 hours covered in the fridge).

Preheat the grill for 15 minutes. Place the chicken wings on the grill and cook for 20 to 25 minutes, or until the chicken is cooked through and caramelized all over.

To cook in the oven, line a tray with foil. Place a rack over the foil and put the wings on the rack.

Cook for 25 to 30 minutes on one side, turn, and cook for another 15 minutes on the other side to ensure they are crisp all over.

To serve the wings, squeeze on fresh lime juice and sprinkle with the coriander, chillies, and onions.

**Top Tips** • **To add smoky flavor, I use the smoke seasoning technique discussed in the Introduction (see Dhunaar, page 12). All you need to do is remove the wings from the oven and place a piece of charcoal on the flame until it starts to get hot. Place the hot charcoal into an old ramekin or on some aluminum foil in the tray of wings.**

**Put 2 green cardamom pods, 2 cloves, and a bay leaf in the ramekin around the hot charcoal, and pour a heaped teaspoon of ghee over the charcoal. This will start to smoke very quickly. Cover the tray of wings with foil for 3 to 4 minutes so they take on the smoky flavor.**

# Hariyali Chicken Tikka Skewers

Tikka, or tikki, just means small, bite-size pieces. Hariyali is a green marinade, but you can also make this dish with a tandoori marinade. The Hariyali marinade uses mint, coriander, and spinach, with some very subtle spices in a yogurt base. I like to use peppers here as well, because it makes the whole dish colorful, and we all know that eating the rainbow is not only fun but good for us too. These skewers are great with rice or a salad, and kids love them in wraps (but you might have to pick out the peppers).

**Serves 4**

MARINADE

1 teaspoon cumin seeds

1 teaspoon coriander seeds

1 bunch fresh coriander, leaves and stems (more to serve)

½ bunch fresh mint leaves

handful of fresh spinach

4 garlic cloves, minced

1-inch (3 cm) piece of fresh ginger

4 fresh green chillies

juice from 1 lemon (more to serve)

1 teaspoon salt

1 teaspoon garam masala

1 teaspoon Kashmiri chilli powder

1 tablespoon (15 ml) mustard oil

3 tablespoons (45 g) Greek yogurt

5 to 6 boneless chicken thighs or 4 boneless chicken breasts, cut into chunks

1 red pepper, cut into chunks

1 yellow pepper, cut into chunks

2 red onions, cut into chunks

Put the cumin and coriander seeds into a pan and toast them until they are fragrant. Crush roughly with a mortar and pestle leave to cool.

Put the coriander, fresh mint, spinach, garlic, ginger, chillies, lemon juice, salt, garam masala, chilli powder, and oil into a blender, and blitz to a smooth paste.

Empty this paste into a bowl, and mix in the yogurt and crushed cumin and coriander seeds.

Combine the chicken, peppers, and onions with the marinade and let it sit for at least 30 minutes (even better if you have more time).

Heat the oven to 400°F (200°C, or gas mark 6). Thread the chicken, peppers, and onions onto six metal or wooden skewers. (If using wooden skewers, soak them in cold water for about 20 minutes before using.)

Cook on a wire rack in the oven for 25 minutes, or on a grill for about 10 to 15 minutes, until cooked through, turning occasionally.

Garnish with coriander and a good squeeze of lemon juice to serve.

# Chicken Momos

Momos are India's answer to the dumpling, inspired by Tibetan dumplings. There is a strong Nepalese influence in Indian cuisine, and this Nepali street food can be found on many Indian street corners. Filled with meat or vegetables, momos are usually flavored with spring onions, fresh coriander, ginger, garlic, chillies, and a few fragrant spices. They are pretty versatile, so you can use minced chicken, pork, lamb, vegetables, or even paneer. Traditionally these are steamed, but you can also pan fry them for a crispy finish.

I have also included a classic momo tomato achaar in the recipe below, but if you prefer, some crispy chilli oil is just as good.

**Makes 12-15**

**MOMO FILLING**

4 to 5 spring or green onions
4 garlic cloves
1 to 2 green chillies
2-inch (5 cm) piece of ginger
1 pound (500 g) ground chicken
1 teaspoon turmeric
1 teaspoon salt or soy sauce
1 teaspoon Kashmiri chilli powder
1 teaspoon coriander seeds, crushed
1 teaspoon cumin seeds, crushed
1 to 2 tablespoons (15 to 30 ml) vegetable oil
handful of fresh coriander leaves

**MOMO WRAPPERS**

2½ cups (300 g) plain flour
pinch of salt
water

**MOMO ACHAAR**

approximately ¾ to 1 cup (200 ml) water
3 large ripe tomatoes, diced
4 to 5 dried Kashmiri chillies
4 garlic cloves
1 tablespoon fresh ginger, grated
1 tablespoon (13 g) sugar
1 tablespoon (15 ml) vinegar
¼ teaspoon salt
1 tablespoon (15 ml) soy sauce

**MOMO FILLING**

Mince the onions with the garlic. Heat a tablespoon of oil in a pan and add the onion mixture; sauté for a few minutes on medium heat.

Mince the ginger and green chillies and add to the pan. Leave to cool for a minute.

Add the mixture to the ground chicken, then add the turmeric, salt (or soy sauce), chilli powder, coriander, and crushed cumin, and mix everything into the meat.

Add 1 to 2 tablespoons of vegetable oil and mix it again. This keeps the mixture nice and juicy.

Add some finely chopped coriander, and mix it all together.

**Top Tip • Vegetarian Momos**
**You can use vegetables of your choice, paneer, or any meat-free product. Just finely grate or chop, and sauté with the onion and garlic mixture to soften the vegetables rather than adding them raw. If it's your first time, try cabbage, pea, and paneer for a simple and delicious momo!**

#### MOMO WRAPPERS

Put the flour and a pinch of salt into a bowl.

Add water, a little at a time, to the flour and stir to make the dough.

Knead the dough for a few more minutes until it is soft and pliable. Let it rest for 20 minutes. Divide the dough into 20 equal pieces.

With a rolling pin, roll the dough as thin as possible into circles. You can also roll it out so it's about 1 mm thick and use a cutter to cut out circles approximately 3 inches (7 to 8 cm) in diameter.

#### MAKE THE MOMOS

Put roughly 1 tablespoon of the filling into the center of each wrapper.

Pleat the edges of the wrapper and rotate until it's pleated and sealed all the way around.

Oil the bottom of your steamer to keep the momos from sticking, and place the momos into the steamer so they are not touching each other.

Steam for 20 to 25 minutes, until the outside is no longer sticky.

#### TO PAN FRY

Add a tablespoon of oil to a sauté pan over medium heat. Add the momos, and once they start to brown, add about ¼ to ½ cup (50 to 100 ml) of water and put the lid on the pan. Let them steam for 10 minutes. (You may need to reduce the heat.)

Remove the lid, and allow the water to evaporate.

Toss the momos in soy sauce and chilli sauce, or in the achaar (recipe to follow).

Momos are great on their own, but sauce takes the taste one step further. In fact, some of the most popular momo shops in Nepal owe it to their unique achaar.

#### MOMO ACHAAR

Heat approximately ¾ to 1 cup (200 ml) of water in a pan and add the diced tomatoes, dried red chillies, garlic cloves, and 1 tablespoon grated ginger, and boil for 10 to 15 minutes until you have a pulp and the garlic is soft.

Pour everything into a blender with sugar, vinegar, salt, and soy sauce and blitz until smooth. Check seasoning, and serve with the momos.

# Lamb Kebabs

Traditionally, kebabs are cooked on long metal skewers in the tandoor oven, but this is my very quick version to cook at home, as a starter or a quick snack. Packed full of flavor, they will always get gobbled up! If you are worried about the spice level, just leave the chillies out.

I am a real advocate for getting the kids cooking, and these lamb kebabs were the first thing my daughter learned to cook all by herself at five years old.

**Makes 8**

- 1 pound (500 g) minced lamb
- 1 medium onion, very finely diced
- 4 garlic cloves, very finely chopped
- 1 tablespoon fresh ginger, grated
- 1 teaspoon salt
- 1 to 2 green chillies, finely chopped
- ½ teaspoon red chilli powder (optional)
- 2 teaspoons cumin seeds, crushed
- 2 teaspoons garam masala
- 1 teaspoon dried fenugreek leaves (kasoori methi)
- handful coriander, finely chopped
- 1 teaspoon oil in a small dish
- 1 red chilli, finely sliced to garnish

Heat the oven to 350°F (180°C, or gas mark 4), line an oven tray with foil, and place a wire rack in the tray.

Place the minced lamb in a large bowl, add all the other ingredients (except the oil and red chilli slices), and mix together using your hands to ensure all the spices are evenly distributed.

Wash hands and rub them with a little oil to help shape the kebabs.

Take a small amount of the mixture and shape it into a small kebab about 4 inches (10 cm) long and 1 inch (3 cm) thick. (Keep them fairly thick, so they stay moist and delicious.)

Place the kebabs on the rack and place the tray in the oven. Cook the kebabs for 15 minutes, remove and turn them, and cook for an additional 10 to 15 minutes. You can leave them for another 5 minutes to brown and crisp up a little.

For an appetizer, serve with crisp salad leaves and thinly sliced onions, with a side of tangy mint chutney. For a snack, stuff in a warmed pita with salad, mint chutney, and a dollop of yogurt.

**Top Tip • These are just as good with beef, pork, or chicken. For some added love, with pork, add 1 teaspoon crushed fennel seeds; with chicken, add finely diced green and red peppers. With beef, add 1 teaspoon paprika.**

# Amritsari Fish Bites

I call these fish fingers with a *pow*! I learned my love for a fish finger sandwich from my dad—his was the best. Whether a frozen fish finger from the supermarket or one of these pakora bites, it has a special place in my heart. The marinade gives the fish a wonderful tang, and the silky gram flour batter is spiked with chillies and carom seeds. Once fried, these are super crispy, and perfect to dip into tomato ketchup as a little snack, in a taco with salad and slaw, or on a bun as a fishwich. I always go for a meaty white fish, but salmon works just as well. The chickpea flour is a great gluten-free alternative to standard breading.

**Makes 15-20**

14 ounces (400 g) white fish loin, cut into large chunks

MARINADE

juice from ½ lime or lemon

1 tablespoon fresh ginger, grated

2 garlic cloves, pounded

1 teaspoon garam masala

½ teaspoon salt

½ teaspoon turmeric

1 chilli, finely chopped (optional)

BATTER

¾ cup (100 g) gram flour, sieved

1 teaspoon carom seeds or cumin seeds

handful coriander, chopped

1 teaspoon baking powder

1 teaspoon chilli powder

½ teaspoon salt

water

rapeseed oil for frying

Remove moisture from the fish by drying on a paper towel.

Make a marinade paste by mixing the lime/lemon juice, ginger, garlic, garam masala, salt, turmeric, and chopped chilli. It should be a dry paste.

Rub the marinade all over the fish and refrigerate for at least 30 minutes (the longer, the better).

Sieve the gram flour into a separate bowl and add carom seeds, coriander, baking powder, chilli powder, salt, and a little water to make a thick batter. Beat to aerate the mixture.

Heat the oil in a wok or karahi to a medium heat. (Note: If the oil is too hot, the batter will cook too quickly and the fish will remain uncooked.)

Dip one of the marinated fish pieces into the batter to cover, and very gently place in the hot oil. Leave to cook for about 3 minutes, using a slotted spoon to move the pakora around.

Once crisp and golden brown, remove and set on paper towels. Taste to check the seasoning, and adjust if required.

Continue to cook the rest in small batches.

**Top Tip • To test if the oil is hot enough, drop a little batter into the oil—if it sinks and starts to sizzle and floats straight up to the surface, the oil is ready.**

# Garlic Chilli King Prawns

**Prawns are widely loved because they are sweet, versatile, and so quick to cook. Always go for the freshest raw prawns you can find, but this recipe also works with frozen prawns. This is a super speedy dish that is perfect for sharing. Just as with Spanish tapas, you need bread to mop up the garlic and chilli sauce—soft, fluffy naan are perfect for this!**

**Serves 4**

1 pound (500 g) shell-on king prawns

1 teaspoon coriander seeds, crushed

½ teaspoon cumin seeds, crushed

½ teaspoon turmeric

½ teaspoon Kashmiri chilli powder

½ teaspoon salt

MASALA

2 tablespoons (30 ml) oil

½ teaspoon brown mustard seeds

½ teaspoon cumin seeds

1 garlic clove, sliced

1 inch (3 cm) piece fresh ginger, julienned

1 chilli, sliced

juice from a lemon

½ teaspoon Kashmiri chilli powder

handful of fresh coriander leaves, chopped

Wash the prawns and pat dry with paper towels.

Sprinkle the crushed coriander and cumin seeds over the prawns with the turmeric, chilli powder, and salt, and mix well. Set to one side for 10 minutes.

Heat the oil in a wide-based pan and add the mustard and cumin seeds. Just as they sizzle, add the sliced garlic, ginger, and fresh chilli.

Quickly stir in the prawns, reduce the heat, and cook for about 2 to 3 minutes.

Squeeze in the lemon juice and add the chilli powder, and toss to coat the prawns. The oil and lemon will create a bit of a sauce.

Once the prawns have turned pink and cooked through (another minute or so), throw in the fresh chopped coriander to serve.

Serve with a lemon wedge and fluffy naan.

# Aloo Pakora Crisps

Potato chips the Indian way—thin or thick slices of potato coated in a gram flour batter and fried to crispy golden discs. These bites are great to dunk into a tamarind chutney, but I also love to put a sprinkling of chaat masala over them for a spicy tang, and a little chilli powder for heat. My mum made these for the kids at every family gathering (leaving out the chillies). In between games of tag, we would surround the table, giggling and dunking them joyfully into tomato ketchup. There were never enough.

**Serves 4**

- ¾ cup (100 g) gram flour, sieved
- 1 tablespoon rice flour
- salt, to taste
- ½ teaspoon carom seeds
- 1 teaspoon cumin seeds
- 1 tablespoon fresh ginger, grated
- ½ teaspoon red chilli powder
- 1 teaspoon garam masala powder
- pinch of fresh coriander, chopped
- ⅔ to ¾ cup (156 to 177 ml) water
- 1 medium potato
- 1 teaspoon chaat masala powder for sprinkling

Mix the flours and spices with the water. Check the seasoning, adjusting if needed. This should be a lovely, thick batter.

Peel and thinly slice the potato into rounds, about 1 inch (3 cm) thick.

Heat the oil for frying in a kadai or large pan on medium heat. You can test the oil is hot enough by dropping in a little batter. If it sizzles and comes to the surface, the oil is ready.

Dip each potato slice in the batter and place it gently in the hot oil. Fry aloo pakoras until they are golden and crisp. They will take 3 to 4 minutes to cook through. If they brown too quickly on the outside, they won't cook through.

Remove from the oil with a slotted spoon and drain on paper towels to remove excess oil.

Repeat with the remaining aloo, cooking in batches.

Sprinkle over chaat masala powder and serve with a mint chutney.

**Top Tip** • **Make a lot!**

# Kashmiri Spiced Halloumi

I love halloumi—who doesn't? But the saltiness of the cheese is just wonderful combined with the warming spices and the heat of the Kashmiri chilli powder in this one. This is great as a snack dipped in a tamarind chutney, on top of a salad (try it with watermelon), or even in a burger with all the trimmings.

**Serves 4**

- 4 garlic cloves, crushed
- 2-inch (5 cm) piece of fresh ginger, grated
- 1 green chilli, finely chopped
- 7 ounces (200 g) halloumi (or paneer or tofu), cut into 2-inch (5 cm) fingers
- 1 tablespoon (15 ml) mustard oil (or rapeseed oil)
- juice of 1 large lemon
- ¾ cup (200 g) Greek yogurt
- 1 teaspoon salt
- 2 teaspoons garam masala
- 1 teaspoon cumin seeds, crushed
- 1 tablespoon Kashmiri red chilli powder
- 1 tablespoon dried fenugreek leaves (kasoori methi)
- handful of fresh coriander leaves, chopped
- 1 lemon, chopped into wedges

Blend the garlic, ginger, and chilli with a mortar and pestle.

Place the halloumi fingers in a dish and stir in the blended ingredients along with the mustard oil and lemon juice.

In a separate dish, mix the remaining ingredients with the yogurt to create a paste.

Add this spiced yogurt paste to the halloumi. Cover and leave to marinade for at least 30 minutes (the longer, the better).

Heat the oven to 350°F (180°C, or gas mark 4).

Transfer to a lined oven tray and cook for about 10 to 15 minutes.

Sprinkle over the chopped coriander and serve with lemon wedges.

**Top Tip • Alternatively, you can cut the halloumi into large cubes; marinate with mushrooms, peppers, and onions; and skewer onto bamboo skewers to cook as kebabs!**

# Nut & Lentil Kofta

No longer are lentils considered a poor man's protein—there are so many new and interesting ways to use them. Whether it's a basic dhal or a spiced fritter, they are a great source of flavor and texture—and easy to cook, too. I have added some basic vegetables to make these kofta bites fun and nutritious. I sometimes put this mixture into a loaf pan, press it down, and bake to make a nut roast, which is a great vegetarian option for Sunday lunch.

**Makes 15-20**

- 1 tablespoon (15 ml) ghee or oil
- 1 teaspoon cumin seeds
- 1 dried chilli
- 1 large onion, finely chopped
- 2 garlic cloves, finely chopped
- 1-inch (3 cm) piece of fresh ginger, grated
- 7 ounces (200 g) chestnut mushrooms, sliced
- 3½ ounces (100 g) paneer, grated
- 1 large carrot, grated
- 1 teaspoon Kashmiri chilli powder
- ½ teaspoon turmeric
- 2 tomatoes, chopped
- 1¼ cups (300 ml) water
- 3½ ounces (100 g) red lentils
- 3½ ounces (100 g) walnuts and cashews, roughly chopped
- 3½ ounces (100 g) mature cheddar cheese, grated
- handful of fresh coriander, chopped
- 2 tablespoons gram flour, toasted in a dry pan

Preheat the oven to 350°F (180°C, or gas mark 4).

Line an oven tray with parchment paper.

Heat the ghee in a large frying pan on medium heat, and add the cumin seeds and dried chilli until sizzling and fragrant.

Add the onion and cook for about 5 minutes, until soft.

Add the garlic and ginger, and stir for a few minutes.

Add the sliced mushrooms and cook until they soften; then stir in the paneer and grated carrot. Cook the mixture for about 3 minutes, and then add the chilli powder and turmeric, cooking for just a minute.

Add the tomatoes and cook for about 1 minute until they start to break down, then add the water and season with salt.

Stir in the lentils and bring to a boil; reduce heat. Leave to simmer over a very gentle heat until all the liquid has been absorbed and the mixture is fairly dry (about 10 minutes). Set aside to cool.

Stir in the roughly chopped nuts with the cheese and coriander. If it feels wet, sprinkle in the toasted gram flour.

Once mixed through, coat your hand in a little oil and make balls the size of golf balls. Place on the oven tray.

Bake for 20 minutes on one side. Turn them and bake for an additional 10 minutes until they are firm when gently pressed.

Serve with a mint chutney.

**Top Tip • Gram flour works to thicken, but it's really important to toast the flour in a dry pan first. It will start to release a sweet aroma once it is toasted. Remove to a bowl to cool or it will burn. To make this recipe vegan, simply replace the ghee with coconut oil and omit the cheese and paneer.**

# Vegetable Samosa

One of India's most famous items is the samosa, and I love how slightly different versions can be found across the globe: In South Africa, it's the samoosa; in Somalia, it's the sambuus; in Iran, it's the sambosa. Whatever you call it, it's a wonderful crisp triangular pastry parcel filled with a spiced mixture. In India, it's usually potato and peas, but you can use a filling of minced lamb, beetroot, and coconut, or even spicy chickpeas. The pastry also varies—some prefer a crisp phyllo style (which you can buy), though I personally find the Punjabi style below much more satisfying.

**Makes 15-20**

**FILLING**

4 potatoes
1 teaspoon rapeseed oil
½ teaspoon cumin seeds
⅓ cup (70 g) frozen peas
1 tablespoon grated ginger
1 teaspoon salt
2 chillies, finely chopped
½ teaspoon chilli powder
1 to 2 teaspoons garam masala
2 tablespoons fresh coriander, chopped

**PASTE**

1 tablespoon plain flour in a small bowl
splash of cold water

**PASTRY**

1½ cups (200 g) plain flour
1½ tablespoons rapeseed oil
pinch of salt
approximately ½ cup (100 ml) water

vegetable oil for frying

**FILLING**

Gently boil the potatoes with the skin on (do not boil too vigorously) for about 25 minutes until soft. Remove from the heat and allow to cool. Once cooled, peel the skin off with your fingers.

Cut the potatoes into small ½-inch (1 cm) cubes and place in a large bowl.

In a small frying pan, heat the oil and fry the cumin seeds. When sizzling, carefully add the peas and gently fry for a few minutes to soften. Remove from the heat and cool before adding to the potatoes.

Add the grated ginger, salt, chillies, chilli powder, garam masala, and fresh coriander to the potatoes and stir. Adjust the seasoning, if desired, and refrigerate for 10 minutes.

**PASTE**

Create flour glue by adding water to the flour to make a thick, sticky paste.

**PASTRY**

Place flour, oil, and salt in a bowl and rub the mixture together.

With your hand, sprinkle in a little water at a time to bring the dough together.

Continue to add the water in this way until the dough forms. Using wet hands, knead the dough until it is soft and no longer sticking to your hands or the bowl.

Refrigerate for 10 minutes. Heat up a tawa (Indian griddle pan) or frying pan on the lowest heat setting.

Take a small tangerine-sized ball of the dough and roll it between your palms to make a smooth ball. Flatten and roll out with a rolling pin to create a thin, round disc the size of a side plate, flouring when

necessary. Place the disc on the tawa for 4 seconds. Remove and place on a chopping board. Using a sharp knife, slice the disc in half so you are left with two semicircles.

**Top Tip** • **Serve hot! My children like samosas with tomato ketchup, but in my opinion the only way to eat samosas is with a tangy tamarind (imlee) chutney.**

### MAKE THE SAMOSA

Place one semicircle on your hand with the flat edge at the top and the cooked side facing you. Dip your finger in the flour paste and spread it across the straight edge.

Fold in the two corners so they meet in the middle ensuring one edge overlaps the other and press together to seal all the way down to create a smooth upside-down cone.

Turn the cone over so the pointed end is at the bottom. Using a spoon, fill the cone with the potato filling to two-thirds of the way up.

Seal the opening with the paste, creating a triangle pastry. Place it on the tray and pat down to even the filling out. Repeat with the remaining dough until you use up all the filling.

### COOK THE SAMOSA

Heat the oil for deep-frying in a large pan. You can test whether it's hot enough by dropping in a little bit of pastry—if it bubbles and floats to the top immediately, the oil is ready.

Very carefully slip one samosa into the hot oil and leave to cook for a few seconds. As the pastry begins to bubble, turn it over using a slotted spoon.

Gently cook until it turns a beautiful golden brown. Remove from the oil and place on paper towels. As you become more confident, fry two or three samosas at the same time.

# 2

# For the Family

Of course, not every meal is a special occasion—in fact, most are just part of the daily rush. In this chapter, I cover a selection of Indian-inspired dishes that I have created for my family, which I hope yours will enjoy as well. It's not every night you want a curry or a full-on Indian meal, but that doesn't mean you can't use those fabulous spices to enhance the aromas and flavor of any dish.

I know that weeknights can be chaos, with everyone coming and going at different times, so I have included a handful of my party tricks to make your life a little easier (without sacrificing any deliciousness!).

# Balti Chicken Pie

**Rich, bold flavors of a delicious north Indian curry are piled high into a pie dish with a yummy pastry crust. The spices and creamy masala are the most perfect filling for a light crisp pastry—although it may seem strange, why not give it a try?**

**Makes 4 individual pies**

1-inch (3 cm) piece of fresh ginger
6 garlic cloves
1½ teaspoons cumin seeds, crushed
1 tablespoon coriander seeds, crushed
2 tomatoes, quartered
1½ teaspoons garam masala
1 teaspoon turmeric
1 teaspoon Kashmiri chilli powder
1 tablespoon (15 g) full-fat Greek yogurt
salt, to taste
2 tablespoons (30 ml) rapeseed oil
1 teaspoon brown mustard seeds
1 bay leaf
1 onion, finely chopped
6 green chillies, chopped (reduce if this is too many for you)
1½ pounds (700 g) boneless chicken thigh fillets, cut into bite-size chunks
7 ounces (200 g) spinach, sliced
black peppercorns, freshly ground
1 tablespoon (15 ml) lemon juice, or to taste
large handful of fresh coriander leaves, finely chopped

**PASTRY**

6 sheets puff pastry
1 egg, whisked
1 teaspoon mustard seeds

In a blender, mince together the ginger and garlic and set to one side.

Grind the cumin and coriander seeds and set to one side.

Blend the tomatoes to a paste and stir in the ground spices, garam masala, turmeric, chilli powder, yogurt, and salt.

Heat the oil in a nonstick saucepan (or karahi, if you have one) on medium heat and add the mustard seeds. Once the mustard seeds pop, add the bay leaf and chopped onion. Stir and cook on medium heat. After 15 minutes, add the minced ginger and garlic with the chopped green chillies for 10 to 20 minutes until the onions are golden. If the onions catch, add a splash of water and continue to cook the onions.

Stir in the blended tomatoes, spices, and yogurt mix. Turn the heat up and stir until the mixture thickens and you are left with a thick masala paste (10 minutes).

Add the chicken pieces and stir into the thick masala to coat it.

Reduce the heat and place the lid on the pan. Leave to cook for about 20 minutes, stirring every now and then.

The chicken will produce a lovely, thick gravy. Once the chicken is cooked through, add the spinach and cook for a few minutes. You can adjust the consistency of the sauce by adding a little hot water to ensure you have enough sauce for the pie. Once cooked, add some black pepper and a squeeze of lemon, and adjust the seasoning, if necessary.

Stir in the chopped coriander and remove the bay leaf.

**PASTRY**

Preheat the oven to 400°F (200°C, or gas mark 6).

Cut out four 5-inch (12 cm) circles from the pastry sheets and push each into a 3½-inch (9 cm) pie tin or ramekin. Divide the filling to fill each pie tin.

Use the remaining pastry to cut out four 4-inch (11 cm) rounds to top the filling. Cover pies with pastry rounds, crimping the edges to seal. Make a hole in the center of each pie. Brush with beaten egg and scatter with mustard seeds. Bake for 20 minutes or until golden.

# Spiced Yogurt Crispy Chicken (Burger)

It has long been a goal of mine to create the best spicy fried chicken out there, and this is where I am in my journey so far: Behold the spiced yogurt fried chicken burger! What makes this recipe even greater is that you can use it for both fried chicken on the bone or for breast pieces to make the crispiest, dirty chicken burger ever!

**Makes 4**

4 skinless, boneless chicken breasts or 4 chicken pieces on the bone if you are making fried chicken

MARINADE

1½ cups (350 g) yogurt

1½ tablespoons (20 ml) milk

4 garlic cloves, minced

1½-inch (4 cm) piece of fresh ginger, grated

juice of 1 lemon

1 green chilli, chopped

2 teaspoons Kashmiri chilli powder

1 teaspoon garam masala

1 teaspoon dried fenugreek leaves (kasoori methi)

COATING

¾ cup (100 g) plain flour

1 tablespoon rice flour or corn flour

2 teaspoons baking powder

1 tablespoon chilli powder

1 teaspoon salt

vegetable oil for frying

DIRTY ADDITIONS

chilli mayo (6 tablespoons [84 g] mayonnaise mixed with 2 tablespoons [30 ml] hot chilli sauce)

4 brioche buns, halved and toasted

iceberg lettuce, shredded

8 rashers of smoked streaky bacon, cooked until crisp

sliced gherkins

slices of chilli cheese

sliced mushrooms sautéed with garlic

If the chicken breasts are large, slice them in half.

Mix all the ingredients for the marinade, add the chicken pieces, and cover. Marinate in the fridge for at least 2 hours but preferably overnight.

Mix the flour with the seasonings in a large, roomy bowl.

Half-fill a large fryer or a pan with vegetable oil and heat to 350°F (180°C). Also heat your oven to 400°F (200°C, or gas mark 6) and prepare a tray with a wire rack.

Mix together all the coating ingredients in a wide bowl. Remove the chicken pieces from the marinade and dredge in the coating, shaking off any excess.

Cook the chicken in the fryer, in batches, for 10 minutes on each side, until deep golden brown.

Drain on paper towels, place on the wire rack, and keep warm in the oven so they stay crisp while you cook the remaining chicken. Ensure the internal temperature of the chicken has reached 165°F (74°C).

If making a chicken burger, smear the chilli mayo on the toasted buns. Add the lettuce, top with the chicken, and add the fillings of your choice.

# Crispy Chicken Bomb with Fenugreek Garlic Butter

Breaded chicken is a favorite for many families. This dish was inspired by a classic breaded chicken breast filled with garlic cream, but I've stuffed it with *methi* (or fenugreek leaf) butter. Fenugreek is also the key ingredient in makhani sauce (what you might know as butter chicken sauce), so I've combined these two delicious elements.

**Makes 4**

**FENUGREEK GARLIC BUTTER**

6 tablespoons (90 g) salted butter, softened

2 teaspoons dried fenugreek leaves (kasoori methi), finely chopped

2 garlic cloves, very finely minced or grated

**CHICKEN BOMB**

1 tablespoon fresh ginger, grated

3 garlic cloves, minced

2 green chillies, finely chopped

14 ounces (400 g) ground chicken

1 teaspoon Kashmiri chilli powder

2 ounces (50 g) cheddar cheese, grated

1 teaspoon cumin seeds

1 teaspoon salt

handful of fresh mint

handful of coriander stems

1 tablespoon (15 ml) oil

2 teaspoons garam masala

1 egg

5 tablespoons (39 g) flour

2 cups (220 g) bread crumbs

**Top Tip • Keep an extra fenugreek garlic butter stick in the freezer. Stuff the butter into a chicken breast before breading it —Chicken Kiev with a Hari twist. These chicken bombs can also be frozen for a quick weeknight dinner.**

**FENUGREEK GARLIC BUTTER**

Place ingredients in a bowl and mix until combined.

Scrape the mixed butter onto a sheet of plastic wrap or parchment paper and roughly shape into a cylinder and place in the freezer until firm.

**CHICKEN BOMB**

Blend the ginger, garlic, and chillies.

Put the ground chicken into a bowl and add the ginger, garlic,and chillies. Sprinkle in the chilli powder, cheese, cumin seeds, and salt.

Very finely chop the mint and coriander stems and mix into the chicken mixture.

Add the oil and garam masala, and mix it all together. Let the mixture rest in the fridge for at least 30 minutes.

Cut the garlic and fenugreek butter into 2-inch (5 cm) discs.

Crack an egg into a bowl and whisk, and put the flour and bread crumbs in two separate wide bowls.

Wet your hands (to prevent the meat from sticking to your fingers), scoop a handful of the ground chicken mixture, and flatten it in your hands. Place the butter disc into the center and roll the mixture into a ball. Repeat with the remaining chicken, wetting your hands between each one. Place the balls in the fridge for 10 minutes to firm up.

Coat the chicken balls in the flour and shake off the excess.

Coat each ball in the whisked egg, dripping off the excess, and then in the bread crumbs, pressing to adhere.

Put the coated chicken balls in the fridge for 30 minutes until firm to handle.

Preheat the oven to 350°F (180°C, or gas mark 4) and place a rack on a tray.

In a wok or small pan, pour oil deep enough to cover the chicken balls. Heat to 375°F (190°C).

Carefully place each chicken bomb into the oil and cook one ball at a time until it turns golden and crispy.

Place the chicken bomb on a rack and bake for 10 minutes. Let the chicken rest for 2 minutes before serving on a bed of butter sauce.

# Tandoori Tray Bake

A tray bake, as we call it in the United Kingdom, is a great way to feed the family in one hit. (They've recently become popular in the United States under the name "sheet pan dinners.") Though beloved for their simplicity, they still need to be super tasty to please everyone. I quite often do tandoori chicken with salad, corn, and potato wedges, but this all-in-one tray bake covers all the bases. Oh, and the roasted lemon adds a zingy sweetness, so make sure you squeeze that over the chicken!

**Serves 4**

MARINADE

1 large lemon
4 garlic cloves, crushed
¾-inch (2 cm) piece of fresh ginger, grated
1 green chilli, finely chopped
¾ cup (200 g) Greek yogurt
1 teaspoon salt
1 teaspoon garam masala
1 teaspoon cumin seeds, crushed
1 tablespoon Kashmiri red chilli powder
1 tablespoon dried fenugreek leaves (kasoori methi)

8 pieces of chicken drumsticks and/or thighs, skinned
1 pound (500 g) new potatoes
2 corns on the cob, cut into 3 pieces
1 red onion, cut into wedges
1 lemon, cut into wedges
1 teaspoon cumin seeds
1 tablespoon (15 ml) mustard oil
salt to taste
1 green pepper, cut into chunks
1 red pepper, cut into chunks

GARNISH

fresh coriander
sliced red onion
red chilli, sliced (optional)

Mix all the marinade ingredients in a bowl so they are fully combined.

Slash the chicken pieces to the bone and place in the bowl with the marinade, fully coating the pieces. Marinate in the fridge as long as possible, overnight if you can.

Preheat the oven to 350°F (180°C, or gas mark 4).

Slice each of the new potatoes halfway down but not all the way through (hassleback) 3 or 4 times, to pick up the flavors while cooking. Place in a large roasting pan with the pieces of corn, onion, and lemon wedges.

Place the marinated chicken in between the vegetables and drizzle over the mustard oil, cumin seeds, and a sprinkling of salt.

Place in the hot oven and bake for 30 minutes. Then add the pepper chunks and cook for an additional 15 to 20 minutes until cooked and the chicken has crisped up.

To serve, sprinkle with coriander, sliced onion, and red chilli slices (optional).

**Top Tip • You can also add mushrooms, paneer, butternut squash, or any other veg of your choice.**

# Spiced Battered Fish

**As a kid we had fish and chips from the chip shop every Friday—it was the only day we got to enjoy a Western meal at home, and it was always a real treat. This dish is a take on classic British fish and chips, but the fish is marinated with north Indian spices. Many people think that white fish is too delicate to work with Indian spices, but tell that to the millions of Indians who enjoy fish every day!**

**Serves 4**

1½-inch (4 cm) piece of fresh ginger
4 garlic cloves
2 lemons
½ teaspoon turmeric powder
1 teaspoon cumin seeds, crushed
1 teaspoon coriander seeds, crushed
1 teaspoon carom seeds (ajwain seeds)
1 teaspoon Kashmiri chilli powder
salt to taste
1½ cups (200 g) gram flour (chickpea flour)
water
14 ounces (400 g) firm white fish in thick portions
oil for deep-frying

Crush the ginger and garlic to a paste with a mortar and pestle and squeeze in the juice from 1 lemon. Add to a large bowl.

Cut the second lemon into wedges to serve with the fish.

Add the turmeric and crushed cumin and coriander seeds to the bowl with the carom seeds, chilli powder, and salt.

Sieve in the gram flour, and mix all the ingredients together, adding a little water to make a thick batter.

Place the fish in the batter and coat all the pieces—marinate for about 30 minutes.

Begin to heat the oil in a fryer to 350°F (180°C). Check if the oil is hot enough by dropping a little batter into the oil. If it bubbles and floats to the top straightaway, it's ready.

Very gently place the battered fish into the oil (place it away from you so the hot oil doesn't splash up).

Fry the fish until it's cooked through and each piece is golden and crispy (about 5 to 6 minutes).

Remove and place on paper towels to drain. Serve hot with home-made chips and a wedge of lemon.

**Top Tip • To make this vegan, use banana blossom (available in cans)—it's the perfect alternative to fish. Coat it in the flour mixture before adding the water. Then simply add the water to make the batter, and coat with the batter and fry in the same way.**

The pleasures of reading morph
into the aesthetic delights of print
and paper. Reading a favourite novel
on a screen is like tasting a vintage
wine through a straw. The unintended
consequence of the ebook, Daunt

# Fennel-Infused Fish Pie with Sweet Potato Chilli Mash

A great midweeker, fish pie embellished with fennel and mustard seeds elevates a standard pie to something spectacular. I have used chilli to balance out the sweetness of the sweet potatoes, but you can replace it with regular creamed potatoes if you prefer.

**Serves 4-6**

2 tablespoons (30 ml) oil
1 teaspoon fennel seeds
½ teaspoon mustard seeds
1 onion, chopped
2 garlic cloves, minced
1 large handful of fresh spinach, chopped
1 chilli, chopped
1¾ cups (400 ml) cream
14 ounces (400 g) firm white fish, cut into large chunks
7 ounces (200 g) salmon, cut into large chunks
3½ ounces (100 g) smoked fish, cut into large chunks
10½ ounces (300 g) prawns
salt and pepper to taste

**TOPPING**

2 or 3 large sweet potatoes, peeled and boiled
1 tablespoon (15 ml) ghee
1 teaspoon garam masala
2 spring or green onions, chopped
3½ ounces (100 g) cheddar cheese, grated
½ teaspoon chilli flakes (more for extra heat)

Preheat the oven to 400°F (200°C, or gas mark 6).

Heat the oil on medium heat in a wide pan and temper the fennel and mustard seeds until they crackle. Add the chopped onion and cook for 5 minutes.

Stir in the garlic and cook through, allowing the onions to soften and turn translucent.

Add the chopped spinach and chilli. Once the spinach has wilted, pour in the cream and stir. Season with salt and pepper.

As the cream warms up, place the fish and prawns into the pan and simmer gently for a few minutes until it's just cooked through.

Remove from the heat and place in a casserole dish.

**TOPPING**

Mash the sweet potatoes and add the ghee, garam masala, and spring onions and stir to combine.

Cover the fish with the potatoes, and sprinkle over the grated cheese and chilli flakes. Bake in the oven for 20 to 25 minutes, until the top is golden and the pie is bubbling.

**Top Tip • Thinly slice a bulb of fennel and layer the bottom of the casserole dish for added texture, crunch, and fennel flavor.**

# Fishcakes with a Vermicelli Crunch

**Fishcakes are a great way to get fish into the weekly meal plan, and my kids loved these. Of course, you can skip the hot stuff, but I find the spices really jazz up standard fishcakes. The vermicelli adds a great crunch as well, but use only the very fine Indian vermicelli—the thick pasta vermicelli will leave your cakes hard-coated in raw pasta. If you can't find the Indian vermicelli, go with bread crumbs instead.**

**Serves 4**

- 10½ ounces (300 g) potatoes, peeled and cubed
- 1 small onion, finely diced
- 1-inch (3 cm) piece of fresh ginger, grated
- 2 garlic cloves, minced
- 2 green chillies
- ½ teaspoon turmeric powder
- 1 teaspoon Kashmiri chilli powder (optional)
- 1 teaspoon coriander seeds, crushed
- handful of fresh coriander stalks, finely chopped
- ½ teaspoon salt, or to taste
- 5 ounces (150 g) salmon, skinned, boned, and chopped
- 9 ounces (250 g) white fish, skinned, boned, and chopped
- wedge of lemon
- 1 tablespoon corn flour
- oil for frying

**COATING**

- 1 cup (140 g) thin vermicelli noodles (not the pasta), crushed
- 2 tablespoons plain flour
- 6 tablespoons (89 ml) water

Boil the potatoes until they are soft, then mash and set to one side.

Heat the oil on medium heat in a pan and add the onions. Sauté until soft, and then add the ginger, garlic, and chillies.

Add all the spices with the coriander stalks and salt, and stir.

Stir in the chopped fish and cook with a squeeze of lemon juice for a few minutes until the fish is cooked through.

Remove the pan from the heat and allow to cool before adding the mashed potatoes with the corn flour. Mix together. Adjust the seasoning if required.

Wet your hands before making about 10 large or 20 small patties out of the mixture, and refrigerate.

In a bowl, mix the flour and water to make a thick batter.

On a tray, crush the vermicelli to small bits (or use a food processor to break it up).

Heat the oil in a pan to fry your cakes.

Place each patty in the batter to coat it on both sides. Use a fork to fish it out and remove any excess batter. Place it on the tray with the vermicelli.

Cover the patty with the vermicelli so it's completely coated, and set to one side. Repeat with all the patties.

Check that the oil is hot, then place as many of the cakes into the pan as will fit. Cook for 2 to 3 minutes, and then turn them over until they are golden and crispy on both sides. Repeat with the remaining fishcakes.

# Aloo Tikki Topped with Tandoori King Prawns

Aloo tikki (or Indian spicy potato cakes) make a great snack on their own and are sold on street corners in India as a quick bite or served with spiced chickpeas as a mini salad. They can be played down as a burger patty or jazzed up as a posh little starter for a special occasion. Try them topped with a juicy marinated king prawn—they will definitely impress.

**Serves 4**

- 12 large uncooked king prawns
- 1-inch (3 cm) piece of fresh ginger
- 2 garlic cloves
- 1 fresh chilli, chopped
- ½ teaspoon chilli powder
- 1 teaspoon salt
- juice of 1 lemon
- ⅓ cup (100 g) yogurt
- 1 teaspoon mustard oil plus 1 tablespoon (15 ml) to cook the prawns
- 1 teaspoon garam masala

**ALOO TIKKI**

- 4 medium potatoes, washed with skin on
- 1 teaspoon salt
- 1 teaspoon garam masala
- 1 teaspoon cumin seeds
- 2 chillies, finely chopped
- 2 tablespoons (16 g) fresh ginger, grated
- handful of fresh coriander leaves, chopped

**GARNISH**

- half a lemon
- handful of coriander, finely chopped

**PRAWNS**

Slice down the back of each prawn and use a toothpick to pull out the dark vein. Wash and dry on paper towels.

Crush the ginger, garlic, and chilli with a mortar and pestle to make a paste.

Place the prawns in a large bowl and sprinkle with the chilli powder, salt, lemon juice, and the crushed ginger and garlic. Set to one side.

Blend the yogurt, 1 teaspoon oil, and garam masala together and add to the prawns. Mix and ensure they are fully coated. Refrigerate until required.

**ALOO TIKKI**

Place the potatoes with the skin on in a pan, cover with cold water, and bring to a boil. Reduce the heat and gently cook until soft. Drain and allow to cool.

Once cooled, peel the skin off with your fingers and discard. Grate the potatoes into a bowl.

Add the salt, garam masala, cumin seeds, chillies, ginger, and coriander, and mix together.

Wet your hands so the potato mixture doesn't stick to your fingers, and begin to shape the potato mixture into small patties or tikki, roughly 1½ to 2 inches (4 to 5 cm) in diameter and about 1 inch (3 cm) thick.

Heat a little oil in a frying pan on medium heat.

Place the cakes in the pan and cook until golden brown on both sides.

Once the tikki are almost cooked, heat 1 tablespoon mustard oil in a frying pan on high heat and fry the prawns for 3 to 4 minutes until they turn pink.

Once the tikki are crisp on both sides, top each with a prawn, and squeeze over lemon juice and fresh coriander to serve.

# Barbecue Pulled Lamb Burger

**If you love a low, slow cook, this is a wonderful way to use lamb shoulder. (You could also use pork butt or beef shin, if you prefer.) The dry rub is a great way to get those smoky flavors penetrating into the joint.**

**Serves 8-10**

**SPICE RUB**

2 tablespoons (36 g) salt

1 tablespoon Kashmiri chilli powder

1 tablespoon cumin seeds, crushed

1 tablespoon coriander seeds, crushed

1 tablespoon (15 g) muscovado brown sugar

4½ pounds (2 kg) lamb shoulder

**SPICY BARBECUE SAUCE**

1 onion, sliced

5 garlic cloves

1½-inch (4 cm) piece of fresh ginger, grated

handful of dried apricots, roughly chopped

7 tablespoons (100 ml) vinegar

⅔ cup (150 ml) orange juice

2 to 4 red chillies, chopped

4 tomatoes, roughly chopped

**TO SERVE**

handful of pomegranate seeds

fresh coriander, chopped

2 red chillies, sliced (optional)

8–10 brioche rolls, toasted

Mix the dry rub ingredients in a bowl.

Score the meat and rub the spice mix all over. Set to one side.

Preheat the oven to 275°F (135°C, or gas mark 1).

Slice the onion and place into an oven tray. Add the garlic, ginger, apricots, vinegar, orange juice, chillies, and tomatoes. Place the lamb on top and cover the tray tightly with foil.

Place it in the oven, and cook for 4 hours.

After 4 hours, remove the foil, take the lamb out, and pour the juices from the tray into a pan.

Place the lamb back in the oven and cook for another 30 minutes.

Heat the juices in the pan, and simmer until thickened.

Pour some of the sauce over the lamb and cook for 10 to 15 minutes more. Remove from the oven and let the meat rest.

You should be able to pull the bone straight out of the lamb shoulder. Shred the lamb using two forks and stir in more of the thickened sauce. Keep some to serve on the side.

Sprinkle over a handful of pomegranate seeds, chopped coriander, and sliced chillies and load onto toasted rolls.

**Top Tip • Try this recipe with different cuts of meat.**

# Bunny Chow

This is South Africa's answer to the curry and a tiffin (a light teatime meal) all in one, and a great example of how food and flavors travel across the globe. It was created by Indian migrant workers in Durban who carried their curry lunches to the field in hollowed loaves of bread.

A classic bunny chow is pretty hot, with a distinctly African curry flavor since the migrants couldn't obtain all the ingredients they needed to re-create the flavors of home.

**Serves 4-6**

- 1 tablespoon (15 ml) rapeseed oil
- 3-inch (7 cm) piece of cassia bark
- 6 green cardamom pods
- 4 cloves
- 1 bay leaf
- 1 teaspoon fennel seeds
- 10 curry leaves
- 1 large onion, finely diced
- 6 garlic cloves, minced
- 1 tablespoon (15 ml) white vinegar
- 2 teaspoons sugar
- 1 tablespoon fresh ginger, grated
- 2 to 4 green chillies, diced
- ½ teaspoon turmeric
- 1 teaspoon garam masala
- 1 teaspoon Kashmiri chilli powder
- 1 teaspoon cumin seeds, ground
- 1 teaspoon coriander seeds, ground
- 2 pounds (1 kg) lamb neck fillet or leg, diced, or 6 chicken thighs (skinned, boned, and chopped)
- 1 teaspoon salt or to taste
- 5 small to medium potatoes, quartered
- 2 tomatoes, puréed
- handful of fresh coriander leaves, chopped

**TO SERVE**

- 4 medium crusty buns

**TOPPINGS (OPTIONAL)**

- chopped tomatoes or tomato kachumber
- sliced red onion rings or Punjabi piyaz
- sliced green chillies
- Greek yogurt or cucumber raita

Heat the oil on medium heat in a pot and add the cassia bark, cardamom, cloves, bay leaf, and fennel seeds, and stir until fragrant.

Add the curry leaves and diced onion. Turn the heat high for a few minutes, stir, and then reduce to a medium heat and cook for 15 to 20 minutes until golden brown.

Add the minced garlic and cook for 3 to 4 minutes.

Stir in the vinegar and sugar, and then add the grated ginger and diced chillies.

Add the turmeric, garam masala, chilli powder, ground cumin, and ground coriander.

Stir in the meat and salt, and coat the meat with the spices.

Cover and cook on low heat for 20 minutes, stirring occasionally.

Add the potatoes and cook for another 20 minutes before adding the pureed tomatoes.

Leave for another 20 minutes until the meat is tender and the potatoes are soft. Remove from the heat and stir in the chopped coriander.

**TO SERVE**

Hollow out the inner part of each bun, keeping it intact.

Scoop the curry into the bunny and serve with tomato kachumber, red onion rings, sliced green chillies, and yogurt or raita on the side.

# Banana Blossom Cutlet

This is exactly what it sounds like: the banana flower, also known as the banana heart. The next vegan diner's dream, it's a purple-skinned flower that grows on the end of a cluster of the banana fruit and looks a bit like an artichoke. The pretty tear-shaped ingredient has been part of Indian and Southeast Asian cuisine for many years. While it can be eaten raw, what makes the blossom spectacular is that when cooked the chunky flesh flakes just like fish; and although it has a neutral taste, its fibrous nature means that it can take on strong flavors and seasoning. You can find it canned, fresh, or frozen.

**Serves 4**

- 1 medium potato
- 14 ounces (400 g) canned banana blossom, chopped
- 1 tablespoon coconut oil
- 1 small onion, diced
- 4 garlic cloves, chopped
- 20 curry leaves
- 1½-inch (4 cm) piece of fresh ginger, grated
- 1 green chilli, chopped
- ½ teaspoon turmeric powder
- 1 teaspoon black pepper, ground
- 1 teaspoon garam masala
- 1 teaspoon salt (or to taste)
- 2 tablespoons (15 g) plain flour
- ½ cup (60 g) bread crumbs
- oil to fry

Boil the potato until it's soft, and then grate it. Set aside for later.

Drain the blossom and roughly chop.

Heat coconut oil in a pan, add the diced onion, and sauté for 5 minutes before adding the garlic.

Stir in the curry leaves and cook until golden. Add the ginger and green chilli, and cook for a few minutes.

Sprinkle in the turmeric and add the chopped banana blossom. Stir and sauté until the mixture dries out.

Add the black pepper with the garam masala and salt. Remove from the heat and allow to cool. Add the grated potato and mix thoroughly.

Once it's cool enough to handle, wet your hands and shape into patties.

Make a thin batter with water and plain flour.

Dip the cutlets in this flour batter to lightly coat, and then coat in the bread crumbs.

Pour enough oil to shallowly cover the bottom of a pan and place over medium to high heat.

Fry the patties on both sides until golden brown. Drain on paper towels. Serve with a mango salsa.

# Keema Pie with Fluffy Spiced Mash & Spring Onions

**There is simply nothing more homey and satisfying than shepherd's pie—and as a bonus, it's a great one-tray meal for the whole family. Filled with succulent meat in a delicious gravy and loads of vegetables and topped with creamy mashed potatoes—for me, it ticks all the boxes except for spice, so I always have mine with a huge dollop of chilli sauce on the side. I thought about how I could add my own little twist, and this recipe is what I came up with. I like to use ground lamb, but pork, chicken, or beef will work just as well.**

**Serves 4**

- 2 tablespoons (30 ml) oil
- 1 onion, finely diced
- 3 garlic cloves, finely chopped
- 14 ounces (400 g) canned plum tomatoes
- 1 tablespoon fresh ginger, grated
- 1 teaspoon cumin seeds, crushed
- 1 teaspoon salt
- ½ teaspoon turmeric
- 1 to 2 chillies, finely chopped (optional)
- 10 mushrooms, quartered
- 1¼ pounds (600 g) lean ground lamb
- 3½ ounces (100 g) frozen peas

**MASALA MASH**

- 7 large Maris Piper or russet potatoes, peeled and chopped into chunks
- ½ teaspoon salt
- 2½ tablespoons (40 g) butter
- 3 tablespoons (45 ml) milk
- 1 teaspoon garam masala

**GARNISH**

- handful of fresh coriander leaves, chopped
- 2 spring or green onions, chopped

Heat the oil on medium heat in a wide-based pan and add the diced onion. Sauté for 5 minutes before adding the garlic. Stir and continue to cook for about 10 minutes until the onions are golden brown in color. If the onion catches, reduce the heat and add a dash of water.

Reduce the heat and add the tomatoes, ginger, cumin, salt, turmeric, and chillies (optional).

Stir together and cook to reduce until the tomatoes break down into the sauce (about 5 minutes). All the ingredients should melt together with the spices, creating the aromatic masala paste.

Turn the heat up, add the mushrooms, and cook for a few minutes before adding the lamb.

Stir to coat the lamb with the sauce. Once coated, reduce the heat and cook for about 15 minutes.

Stir in the frozen peas and cook for an additional 5 minutes.

Remove from the heat and spoon into a casserole dish. Allow to cool.

**MASALA MASH**

Preheat your oven to 350°F (180°C, or gas mark 4). Cover the potatoes with cold water and add a little salt. Bring this to a boil, and then reduce the heat. Cook the potatoes until soft. Once cooked, drain and place back in the pan.

Add a little salt and butter and pour in a little milk (add more if required) and mash the potatoes to create a firm mash.

Sprinkle in the garam masala.

Place the masala mash on top of the lamb mixture and place in the oven. Bake for about 25 to 30 minutes until it's bubbling.

To serve, sprinkle with fresh coriander and chopped spring onions.

# Steak 'n' Spice

**If you love your steak with a dash of Tabasco, then you are going to *love* this. It's a superb way to introduce an Indian twist to steak, a lamb chop, or a pork joint. Happily, this is also one of those recipes that makes life easy. Gentle spicing tenderizes the meat and beautifully flavors it at the same time, a bit like the galavat technique (page 13) discussed in the Introduction. All you need to serve this is a luxurious side salad and thick-cut chips.**

**Serves 2**

- 1 tablespoon fresh ginger, grated
- 1 small onion, roughly chopped
- 3 garlic cloves
- 2 teaspoons coriander seeds
- 1 teaspoon cumin seeds
- 1 teaspoon black mustard seeds
- 1 teaspoon Kashmiri chilli powder
- 1 teaspoon salt
- 3 tablespoons (45 ml) vegetable oil
- 2 rib eye steaks
- 1 tablespoon (14 g) butter

Place the ginger, onion, and garlic in a food processor and blend until it's finely minced.

Grind the coriander, cumin, and mustard seeds in a spice grinder. Stir in the chilli powder and salt.

Heat 1 tablespoon (15 ml) of oil over medium heat and add the onion mixture. Sauté gently for 2 to 3 minutes. Remove from the heat and add the ground spices. Mix through until fragrant.

Once cooled, smear the onion and spice mixture over the steaks. Cover in plastic wrap and refrigerate for up to 24 hours.

To cook the steaks, heat a pan or griddle on high heat and place the steaks in the pan. Reduce the heat to medium so the spices don't burn and sear for 2 to 3 minutes, turn them over, and add some butter. Cook to the desired level.

When the steaks are cooked, remove from the heat and let them stand for 5 to 6 minutes.

Thinly slice the steak against the grain to serve.

# Pepperoni Naanza

**A slight Indian twist on a classic Italian pizza. A basic naan dough that includes a sprinkling of turmeric goodness with peppery kalongi seeds makes the base vibrant yellow and crisp. It's dressed with a full-flavored tomato masala and then topped with all the usual favorites.**

**Makes 4**

1 teaspoon dried active yeast
1 teaspoon sugar
1¾ cups (200 g) plain flour
1 teaspoon black onion seeds
½ teaspoon salt
½ teaspoon baking powder
½ teaspoon turmeric
1 tablespoon (15 ml) vegetable oil
2 tablespoons (30 g) plain yogurt
2 tablespoons (30 ml) milk

MASALA

2 tablespoons (30 ml) oil
2 onions, finely diced
1 teaspoon salt
1 heaped tablespoon fresh ginger, grated
1 chilli, finely chopped (optional)
3 garlic cloves, finely chopped
14 ounces (400 g) canned plum tomatoes, puréed
1 teaspoon turmeric
1 teaspoon chilli powder
1 teaspoon garam masala
handful of fresh coriander leaves, chopped

TOPPINGS (OPTIONAL)

shredded mozzarella
diced paneer
shredded cheddar cheese
pepperoni slices
red onion, sliced
black olives
red chilli, sliced
coriander, chopped

In a small bowl, mix the yeast and sugar with a tablespoon of warm water to activate. Leave for 5 minutes in a warm place until frothy.

Meanwhile, in a separate bowl, mix the flour, onion seeds, salt, baking powder, and turmeric. When the yeast is frothy, add it to the flour with the oil and yogurt.

Knead the dough with slightly wet hands, folding as you go, or use a stand mixer if you prefer. If it feels a little dry, add some milk and continue to knead. Once it's nice and soft, cover with plastic wrap and leave it in a warm place to rise for at least 1 hour.

**MASALA**

Heat the oil in a pan on high heat and add the diced onions. Sauté and stir—if it starts to stick, just add a little water and stir. Add the salt to help the onions cook.

Put the ginger, chilli, and garlic into a blender and blend to a paste (add a little water if required).

After 10 minutes of cooking, the onions should have started to brown. Now stir in the ginger, chilli, and garlic paste.

Once softened, add the puréed canned tomatoes and increase the heat until the tomatoes start to simmer.

Reduce the heat and add the turmeric, chilli powder, and garam masala. Cook until the masala is thick.

**MAKE THE NAANZA**

Preheat the oven to 400°F (200°C, or gas mark 6) and insert an oven tray or pizza stone to heat up.

Divide the dough into four balls, and place on a floured surface. Roll each into a tear shape, about ¼ inch (0.5 cm) thick.

Transfer to the hot baking tray and work quickly, smearing on the masala sauce, sprinkling over the cheese, and then adding the toppings of your choice. Top off with a little more cheese.

Place in the oven to cook until the dough turns golden and the cheese bubbles (2 to 5 minutes). Sprinkle with coriander and serve.

# Curried Butternut Squash Soup

Rich, creamy, and full of flavor—soup fans will love this because it is packed with the natural sweet goodness of winter squash, and with a little chilli, it warms you from the inside out. It's the perfect fall family pleaser, but it also makes a great little starter for a party. This recipe works beautifully with pumpkin too.

**Serves 2 as a main dish or 4 as a starter**

- 1 butternut squash
- 1 teaspoon cumin seeds
- 1 red onion, chopped
- 2 garlic cloves, minced
- 1-inch (3 cm) piece of fresh ginger, grated
- 2 red chillies, chopped (keep some for garnish)
- 2 cups (500 ml) chicken stock or water
- 4 tablespoons (50 g) coconut cream

Preheat the oven to 350°F (180°C, or gas mark 4).

Slice the squash into four long strips, remove the seeds, and place on a tray with a little knob of butter on each. Roast in the oven for about 35 minutes until soft.

Meanwhile, heat the oil in a pan over medium heat and add the cumin seeds, stirring until fragrant. Then add the onions and gently cook until soft.

Stir in the garlic, ginger, and chillies and cook for about 5 minutes.

Once the squash is soft, scrape the flesh out and discard the skin. Stir the flesh into the onions.

Add the stock and cook through until everything is soft (about 5 minutes).

Using a hand blender or immersion blender, blitz the soup until it's smooth and thick. Pour in the coconut cream. If it's too thick, add a little hot water.

Pour into bowls and top with a swirl of coconut cream and a chopped chilli. Serve with some crisp naan bread.

**Top Tip • You can use the seeds from the squash or pumpkin as a spiced topper for your soup: Remove the seeds from one pumpkin; wash and dry them on paper towels. Spread the seeds on an oven tray and pour 2 teaspoons of oil over them. Rub to coat them with the oil and sprinkle with 1 teaspoon each of salt and chilli flakes. Roast in the oven for 10 minutes at 350°F (180°C, or gas mark 4) until they are golden brown. After they have cooled, store in an airtight jar and use as needed.**

# Dhal & Aubergine Moussaka

**A classic Greek moussaka is made with spiced lamb and sliced eggplant, but by substituting black lentils for the meat, you can make a wonderfully versatile vegetarian option. The lentils not only add texture, but they soak up the aromatics of the ginger, garlic, and nutmeg. I have added a few extra spices that also combine well with the earthy nature of the lentils.**

**Serves 4-6**

**LENTIL MASALA**

- 1 to 2 tablespoons (15 to 30 ml) vegetable oil
- 1 stick of cassia bark
- 1 teaspoon cumin seeds
- 1 medium onion, finely chopped
- 3 garlic cloves, sliced
- 3 fresh tomatoes, chopped
- 1-inch (3 cm) piece of fresh ginger, grated
- 2 green chillies, chopped
- ½ teaspoon turmeric powder
- 1 teaspoon chilli powder
- 2 teaspoons coriander seeds, crushed
- 3½ ounces (100 g) soaked uncooked urad dhal (whole black lentils) or 14 ounces (400 g) precooked lentils
- salt to taste
- 1 to 2 tablespoons (14 to 28 g) butter
- 1 teaspoon garam masala
- ½ teaspoon nutmeg
- 1 teaspoon dried fenugreek leaf (kasoori methi)
- handful of fresh coriander leaves, chopped

Heat the oil in a pressure cooker (if using uncooked lentils), and add the cassia bark and cumin seeds. When the cumin seeds sizzle, add the chopped onions and garlic. On medium heat, fry until golden brown.

Stir in the chopped tomatoes, ginger, green chillies, turmeric, chilli powder, and crushed coriander seeds.

Stir in 3½ ounces (100 g) of the soaked urad dhal (whole black lentils) and pour in 2 cups (500 ml) of water with a teaspoon of salt (or to taste).

Put the lid on and bring the temperature to high. Reduce the heat and simmer for 25 minutes. (If using cooked lentils, simmer until heated through.)

Turn the heat off and allow the pressure to subside. Remove the lid and stir. Test that the lentils are cooked through (they should be soft and squeeze between your fingers).

If the lentils are still watery, simmer and stir on a gentle heat until they thicken and start to get creamy.

Remove from the heat and take out the cassia bark. Stir in the butter, garam masala, nutmeg, and fenugreek leaf.

Stir in the fresh coriander leaves and set to one side.

Preheat the oven to 350°F (180°C, or gas mark 4).

**CUMIN-GRIDDLED EGGPLANT**

As the lentils are cooking, heat a griddle on high heat.

Mix the crushed cumin seeds with the oil. Drizzle over the eggplant slices and cook on the griddle until they begin to color and soften.

**TURMERIC BECHAMEL**

In a large saucepan, heat butter over medium-high heat until melted.

Stir in flour, turmeric, salt, and pepper. Cook until golden.

Gradually pour in the warmed milk, whisking continuously. Continue cooking, stirring occasionally, over medium heat for 5 to 7 minutes.

*continued next page* ▸

# Dhal & Aubergine Moussaka, continued

**CUMIN-GRIDDLED EGGPLANT**

4 medium eggplants, sliced in 2-inch (5 cm) rings (you could use 2 eggplants and 2 potatoes)

2 tablespoons (30 ml) rapeseed oil

1 teaspoon cumin seeds, crushed

**TURMERIC BECHAMEL SAUCE**

½ cup (120 g, or 1 stick) butter

1 cup (120 g) plain flour

½ teaspoon turmeric

1 teaspoon salt

½ teaspoon fresh ground pepper

4¼ cups (1 L) milk, warmed

¼ teaspoon fresh ground nutmeg

2 large eggs

**TOPPINGS (OPTIONAL)**

sliced red onions

sliced red chillies

Whisk the eggs and pour into the bechamel mixture while stirring. Add the nutmeg.

Continue to stir and bring it to a gentle boil for 2 minutes. Taste and adjust the salt—it's really important that the bechamel is well seasoned.

Remove from the heat and allow to cool and thicken a little more (you should have a heavy, creamy, thick, smooth bechamel sauce).

**ASSEMBLE AND BAKE**

Butter a casserole dish and place half the griddled eggplant in the bottom, top with half the lentil mixture, and smooth it out.

Layer the remaining griddled eggplant on top and add the remaining lentils.

Pour the bechamel sauce on top, smooth it out, and sprinkle over sliced red onions and red chillies (if using).

Place the moussaka on the middle rack of your heated oven. Bake for 45 minutes or until the top turns golden brown.

Remove from the heat and let sit for at least 20 minutes before cutting and serving.

**Top Tip • Red or brown lentils can also be used. They cook more quickly and you don't need a pressure cooker for them. To add bulk, include a layer of sliced potatoes or griddled zucchini.**

# Ricotta-Stuffed Pasta in Saag Masala

**Growing up, we used to eat pasta with a spiced Indian tomato masala and lots of mixed vegetables. Mum didn't really know how to cook it the Italian way, so she improvised with the flavors she understood, and this is one of those dishes. Today pasta is commonplace in India; they love it with a spiced twist.**

**Serves 4**

9 ounces (250 g) giant pasta shells

**TOMATO MASALA**

- 2 tablespoons (30 ml) oil
- 1 teaspoon cumin seeds
- 4 garlic cloves, chopped
- 28 ounces (800 g) canned tomatoes
- 1 tablespoon (16 g) tomato purée
- 2 green chillies, chopped
- ½ teaspoon salt
- ½ teaspoon turmeric
- 14 ounces (400 g) fresh spinach

**RICOTTA SAUCE**

- 9 ounces (250 g) ricotta cheese
- 3½ ounces (100 g) mozzarella cheese, grated
- 2 ounces (50 g) Parmesan cheese, grated
- sea salt and freshly ground pepper

**TOPPINGS**

- 5¼ ounces (150 g) mozzarella cheese, grated
- 1 teaspoon red chilli flakes (optional)
- half a red onion, thinly sliced

**GARNISH**

- handful of fresh coriander leaves, chopped

Cook the pasta in plenty of salted, boiling water for 10 minutes, until just cooked. Drain, rinse under cold water, and set aside.

Heat the oil in a pan on medium heat, add the cumin seeds, stirring until fragrant, and then add the garlic.

Stir and add the tomatoes and tomato purée. Mix in the chillies, salt, and turmeric and simmer until the sauce thickens, about 20 minutes.

Mix together all the ingredients for the ricotta sauce.

Fill each of the cooked shells with the ricotta mixture.

Once the tomato sauce has thickened, stir in the spinach and cook for a minute or two. Pour the tomato masala into a casserole dish.

Preheat the oven to 400°F (200°C, or gas mark 6).

Place the filled pasta shells into the tomato masala and top with the remaining mozzarella cheese, red chilli flakes, and sliced red onion.

Bake in the oven for 15 minutes or until the cheese is golden and bubbling.

Sprinkle over the fresh chopped coriander, and serve with garlic bread.

# 3

# Cheeky Curries

There's nothing more satisfying than a curry! Each dish is a unique experience. I've included several different flavor profiles here, hoping to show you how you can put spices and ingredients together in different formats to reveal the many layers of curry complexity.

# Lamb Balti

**Bold and brash is the only way to describe a balti, which is said to have originated in the United Kingdom by Indian migrants who worked in curry houses in the 1970s. The balti is actually the name of the dish it's cooked and served in; it's made of aluminum and has two handles similar to that of a cast-iron karahi. Serve with a fluffy naan to mop up the delicious sauce.**

**Serves 4-6**

- 1½ teaspoons cumin seeds
- 1 tablespoon coriander seeds
- 1-inch (3 cm) piece of fresh ginger
- 6 garlic cloves
- 2 tomatoes, quartered
- 1½ teaspoons garam masala
- 1½ teaspoons turmeric
- 1 teaspoon Kashmiri chilli powder
- 1 tablespoon (15 g) full-fat Greek yogurt
- salt, to taste
- 2 tablespoons (30 ml) rapeseed oil
- 1 teaspoon brown mustard seeds
- 1 bay leaf
- 1 onion, finely chopped
- 6 to 10 whole green chillies (reduce if this is too many for you)
- 1¼ pounds (600 g) lamb neck fillet, cut into 1-inch (3 cm) pieces
- 1 teaspoon black peppercorns, freshly ground
- 1 tablespoon (15 ml) lemon juice, or to taste
- large handful of fresh coriander leaves, finely chopped

Grind the cumin and coriander seeds, and set aside. Crush the ginger and garlic with a mortar and pestle.

Blend the tomatoes to a purée and stir in the ground spices, garam masala, turmeric, chilli powder, yogurt, and salt.

Heat the oil in a nonstick saucepan (or karahi) and add the mustard seeds. Once they pop, add the bay leaf and chopped onion. Stir and cook on medium heat.

After about 15 minutes, add the crushed ginger and garlic with the green chillies, and cook for at least 20 minutes until the onions are well browned. If the onions catch, add a splash of water and continue to cook.

Stir in the tomato mixture. Turn the heat up and stir until the sauce thickens and you are left with a thick masala paste (10 to 15 minutes).

Add the lamb pieces, coating with the masala. Reduce the heat and place the lid on the pan. Cook for about 40 minutes, stirring occasionally.

The meat will produce a thick gravy. Add a little hot water to loosen it, or stir-fry on high heat to thicken further, depending on how you like it.

Once the meat is tender, add black pepper and a squeeze of lemon.

Check the seasoning and stir in the chopped coriander. Serve with fresh naan (page 92).

# Bhuna Gosht

**This dish is named after the traditional cooking method used to make it. It uses a cacophony of whole spices that are toasted to heighten their aromatics and blended to create a delicious mix. The "bhun" comes at the end of the cooking process, where the masala is reduced on high heat and continually stirred to intensify the flavors. This requires a little elbow grease, so be prepared to work for your supper.**

**Serves 4–6**

2 pounds (900 g) leg of lamb or mutton, trimmed and chopped

SPICE BLEND

2 teaspoons cumin seeds
3 teaspoons coriander seeds
2 teaspoons mustard seeds
2 teaspoons fennel seeds
1 teaspoon fenugreek seeds
2 to 3 dried red chillies

MASALA

1 tablespoon (15 ml) rapeseed oil
2 onions, finely chopped
6 garlic cloves, finely chopped
20 curry leaves
1½-inch (4 cm) piece of fresh ginger, grated
2 to 3 green chillies, sliced in half (optional)
14 ounces (400 g) canned plum tomatoes
1 teaspoon salt
½ teaspoon turmeric
1 teaspoon garam masala
handful of fresh coriander leaves, chopped

Heat a frying pan over medium heat and add the cumin, coriander, mustard, fennel, and fenugreek seeds, and the dried chillies. Keep the spices moving for a minute or two until they become aromatic. Empty the spices into a bowl and let them cool before grinding to a fine powder in a coffee grinder or with a mortar and pestle. Set aside.

Heat the oil and onions in a large pan over high heat, adding the garlic after a few minutes. Sauté and if they stick, add a little water and continue to stir when required.

Once they have browned, add the curry leaves, ginger, green chillies (if using), tomatoes, and salt. Cook until the tomatoes break down, creating a thick paste.

Add the roasted spice mix and turmeric to the pan and stir well. Cook for a minute or two, taking care not to let the sauce catch on the bottom of the pan. If it feels dry, add a splash of water and quickly stir.

Place the meat in the pan and stir to coat on high heat, stir-frying for 5 minutes.

Reduce the heat, put a lid on the pan, and simmer for about 30 to 40 minutes (longer if using mutton). Check that the meat is tender. If it isn't, let it cook a while longer.

When the meat is ready, remove the lid from the pan, turn up the heat, and fry to reduce the sauce until it almost disappears. The aim is to intensify the flavor, creating a dry, concentrated sauce that clings tightly to the tender morsels of meat.

Finish with a sprinkle of garam masala and a handful of chopped fresh coriander.

**Top Tip • This dish is great with more heat, so feel free to add more fresh chillies to make it hotter, if you wish.**

# Thari Wala Chicken

This is my go-to everyday curry. The first thing I learned to cook, it's rustic, homey, and the perfect dish for the whole family to enjoy. It's a versatile base masala that can be used in so many different ways. For me, it represents everything that is great about Indian food. The key is to allow your onions to brown until they are dark and moody brown in color!

**Serves 4-6**

8 to 10 pieces of chicken (4 to 5 legs cut into thighs and drumsticks)

TOMATO MASALA

- 2 tablespoons (30 ml) oil
- 2 onions, finely diced
- 3 garlic cloves, finely chopped
- 14 ounces (400 g) canned plum tomatoes
- 1 heaped tablespoon fresh ginger, grated
- 1 teaspoon salt
- 1 teaspoon turmeric
- handful of fresh coriander stalks, finely chopped
- 1 chilli, finely chopped
- 1 teaspoon of garam masala
- handful of fresh coriander leaves, chopped

Skin the chicken, removing any excess fat. Set aside.

Heat the oil in a pan and add the onions and garlic. Fry on high heat for a few minutes, and then reduce the heat and cook gently for about 20 to 30 minutes until they turn a lovely dark golden brown.

Once the onions are browned, add the canned tomatoes, ginger, salt, turmeric, coriander stalks, and chopped chilli. Increase the heat to high until it comes to a simmer, and then reduce to medium.

Let the onions and tomatoes melt together so they create a thick aromatic masala paste. This will take 5 to 10 minutes, so be patient!

Once the paste is shiny and thick and all the moisture has evaporated, add the chicken pieces and stir to coat.

Fry the chicken on high for 5 minutes.

Reduce the heat to the lowest setting and put the lid on the pan. Cook for 20 to 25 minutes until the chicken is cooked through and the meat is starting to fall away from the bone.

The meat will have created its own thick sauce. Either leave as is or if you like more sauce (like me), add enough boiling water to just cover the chicken and simmer for a few more minutes. Remove from the heat.

Stir in the garam masala and coriander leaves, and serve.

**Top Tips**

- **Make the tomato masala in bulk and freeze in tubs for use during the week.**
- **Use chopped thigh fillets for a boneless version.**
- **Any meat of your choice will work with this masala.**
- **Add coconut milk for a creamy finish.**
- **Add tamarind for a tangy finish.**

**If the onions stick to the bottom of the pan, reduce the heat and add a dash of water. You can do this as many times as you need to. It also helps the onions to start breaking down.**

# Lamb Dhansak

This is a rustic one-pot lamb, lentil, and vegetable stew that's taken to new heights with the use of tangy tamarind and warming spices. Light, sweet, and savory, it's typically eaten with the whole family as a weekend meal.

**Serves 4–6**

LENTIL AND VEGETABLE MIXTURE

2 ounces (60 g) toor dhal (split pigeon peas)

2 ounces (60 g) masoor dhal (split red lentils)

2 ounces (60 g) urad dhal (split and dehusked black lentils)

1 small eggplant, chopped into large chunks

½ small pumpkin, chopped into large chunks (you could also use butternut squash or sweet potato)

1 medium onion, chopped in chunks

15 fresh mint leaves, chopped

DRY SPICES

1 teaspoon cumin seeds

1 teaspoon coriander seeds

1½-inch (4 cm) stick of cassia bark

4 green cardamom pods

4 whole black peppercorns

1 tablespoon dry fenugreek leaves

WET PASTE

6 garlic cloves

1-inch (3 cm) piece of fresh ginger

2 chillies

MASALA

2 tablespoons (30 ml) oil

2 medium onions, diced

1 teaspoon turmeric powder

3 tomatoes, diced

1 tablespoon (15 g) tamarind paste

1 teaspoon salt

1 pound (500 g) leg of lamb, trimmed and cut into chunks

handful of fresh coriander leaves, chopped

LENTIL AND VEGETABLE MIXTURE

Put all the lentils, vegetables, onions, and mint into a pan with 4¼ cups (1 L) of water and some salt. Bring this to a boil, and then simmer for 20 minutes until the lentils have cooked through.

DRY SPICES AND WET PASTE

Place all the dry spices into a spice grinder and blend to a fine powder.

Place this powder into a blender with the garlic, ginger, and chillies and grind to make an aromatic paste. Add a splash of water to loosen if required.

MASALA

Heat the oil over medium heat and fry the diced onions until they are golden brown (about 20 minutes).

Once the onions are browned, add the spice paste along with the turmeric and fry for a few minutes until golden.

Add the tomatoes, tamarind paste, and salt. Stir for about 5 minutes until the masala is thick and glossy.

On high heat, stir in the lamb and coat with the masala. After about 5 minutes, add the cooked lentil mixture and simmer on low heat for about 30 to 40 minutes. Make sure you occasionally stir as this can stick to the bottom of the pan.

Once the meat is tender, check the seasoning and adjust if required.

Sprinkle with the fresh coriander to serve.

# Butter Chicken

Also called Murgh Makhani, this beloved dish is perfect for a weeknight family dinner. The sauce is rich, with a wonderfully creamy, smooth texture as well as an iconic vibrant orange color. There are so many different ways to cook this dish. You can change the recipe to make it healthier if you choose, but assuming you're not eating it every night, I believe it's better to indulge a little! You can also marinate the chicken first—just use the marinade from my Schmokin' Tandoori Wings recipe on page 16.

**Serves 4–6**

TOMATO SAUCE

- 2 medium red onions, roughly chopped
- 2 to 3 green chillies
- 1 teaspoon fresh ginger, grated
- 4 garlic cloves, roughly chopped
- 1½-inch (4 cm) stick of cassia bark
- 4 green cardamom pods
- 3 cloves
- 5 whole black peppercorns
- 1 teaspoon salt
- 7 ripe red tomatoes, roughly chopped, or 14 ounces (400 g) canned plum tomatoes

MASALA

- 2 tablespoons (30 ml) ghee or butter
- 1 tablespoon cumin seeds
- ½ teaspoon turmeric
- 1 teaspoon Kashmiri chilli powder
- 2 teaspoons coriander seeds, crushed (coriander powder)
- 8 chicken thighs or 4 breasts, skinned, trimmed, and cut into cubes
- 1 cup (240 ml) hot water
- 1 tablespoon honey
- ½ cup (100 ml) double cream, heavy cream, or yogurt
- 1 heaped tablespoon dried fenugreek leaves (kasoori methi)
- 1 tablespoon (15 g) butter

TOMATO SAUCE

Put the onions, chillies, ginger, garlic, cassia bark, green cardamom, cloves, peppercorns, and salt into a pan and cover with approximately 2 cups (500 ml) of water. Bring to a boil.

Add the tomatoes and simmer for 15 to 20 minutes on medium heat, stirring occasionally.

After the sauce has reduced and the mixture has thickened, remove the pan from the heat. Remove the cassia bark and let the mixture cool.

Blend to a fine sauce using a hand blender or immersion blender until it's smooth, thick, and creamy.

MASALA

In a second pan, heat the ghee or butter. Once melted, add the cumin seeds and as soon as you can smell the musky cumin aroma, reduce the heat and stir in the tomato sauce. Be very careful as this will spit and bubble so keep stirring. Cook for about 5 to 10 minutes until the butter and sauce come together.

Stir in turmeric, chilli powder, and crushed coriander seeds, and cook for 2 to 3 minutes. Reduce the heat and add the chicken to the pan, stir to coat, and simmer for 15 minutes on a gentle heat.

Add a little hot water to loosen, if required, and then add the honey. Cook for 5 minutes until the chicken is cooked through—the gravy should be a lovely bright orange color.

Remove from the heat and stir in the cream (or yogurt) and fenugreek.

Add a bit of butter or cream on top before serving.

**Top Tip • Make it vegetarian with paneer and peppers! Do not substitute Kasoori methi for the spice—it will be too overpowering; instead add a teaspoon of garam masala.**

# Chettinad Chicken

A lovely, flavorful chicken curry dish from Tamil Nadu in South India, Chettinad Chicken is made by toasting spices with coconut and producing an aromatic masala that has a slight aniseed scent. If too fiery, just reduce the number of dried chillies. This dish would traditionally be served with dosa (crispy lentil pancakes) or appams (rice pancakes), but it is just as good with plain boiled rice.

**Serves 4-6**

- 1 tablespoon poppy seeds
- 1 teaspoon coriander seeds
- 1 teaspoon cumin seeds
- 1 teaspoon fennel seeds
- 3 dried red chillies
- 1-inch (3 cm) stick of cinnamon
- 2 cardamom pods
- 3 cloves
- 9 tablespoons (50 g) grated coconut
- 2 garlic cloves, crushed
- 2 teaspoons grated ginger
- 2 tablespoons (30 ml) oil
- 10 curry leaves
- 2 onions, thinly sliced
- 1 star anise
- 2 tomatoes, diced
- ½ teaspoon turmeric
- 1 teaspoon chilli powder
- salt to taste
- 8 chicken thighs, skinned
- 2 limes, cut in halves
- handful of fresh coriander leaves, chopped

Gently heat a frying pan on medium to low heat and roast the poppy, coriander, cumin, and fennel seeds; dried red chillies; cinnamon; cardamom; cloves; and coconut for 3 to 4 minutes.

Remove from the heat, transfer to a bowl, and let cool.

Once cooled, grind to a fine powder in a spice grinder.

Crush the garlic and ginger with a mortar and pestle and set aside.

In a large pan, heat the oil on medium heat and add the curry leaves. When they stop sputtering, add the sliced onions and fry until light brown. Add the crushed garlic and ginger.

Add the star anise and fry, then stir in the ground spices for a minute before adding a splash of water.

Add the diced tomatoes, turmeric, chilli powder, and salt. Cook for 10 minutes, allowing the tomatoes to break down.

Add the chicken and stir to coat with the sauce. Cover and simmer on the lowest setting until the chicken is tender, about 25 minutes.

Once the chicken is cooked through, squeeze in the juice from the limes, and remove from the heat.

Sprinkle on the fresh coriander leaves and serve.

# Keralan Pork

Pork is not a primary meat for many Indians, but there are some South Indian states where it's considered a delicacy. I think it's a great protein, as it easily carries flavors and works well with spices. Depending on the cut, it can be slow-cooked for a deep, rich curry or you can make a quick, easy meal with loin steaks. It is also a lean meat, once trimmed. Pork and fennel are great friends, and the coconut milk makes a wonderful, velvety masala. Add green beans, baby corn, or red pepper for color and vibrancy.

**Serves 4–6**

- 1⅓ to 2 pounds (600 g to 900 g) pork loin steaks or fillets
- sea salt to taste
- freshly ground black pepper
- 1 teaspoon ground turmeric (separated)
- 2 tablespoons (30 ml) coconut oil
- 1 teaspoon fennel seeds or 2 star anise
- 2 dried red chillies
- 2 onions, finely diced
- 5 garlic cloves, minced
- 14 ounces (400 g) canned tomatoes
- 1 tablespoon (15 g) tamarind paste
- 2 fresh green chillies, chopped
- 1 tablespoon fresh ginger, grated
- 2 teaspoons cumin seeds
- 1 teaspoon coriander seeds
- approximately 1 cup (200 g) coconut cream
- 3½ ounces (100 g) green beans, trimmed
- handful of fresh coriander leaves, chopped

Remove the fat from the pork and cut into strips. Season the pork with salt and lots of black pepper and ½ teaspoon of the turmeric.

Heat a wide pan on medium heat and add the oil. Once hot, add the whole fennel seeds and red chillies.

Add the onions and sauté until they start to brown, then add the minced garlic.

Add the canned tomatoes, tamarind paste, green chillies, and grated ginger and stir to combine.

Grind the cumin and coriander with a mortar and pestle.

Once the masala starts to simmer, add the remaining turmeric, and ground cumin and coriander, and stir. Let it reduce and thicken.

Add the pork and stir to coat with the sauce. Reduce the heat and cook for 5 to 10 minutes.

Pour in the coconut cream and heat through. Then add the trimmed beans and cook for an additional 5 minutes until the beans are tender.

When the pork is cooked through, check the seasoning, add the coriander leaves, and serve with plain rice.

# Nariyal Chicken

**This is a hybrid dish, with a base sauce from the north but using flavors from the south. It is one of my personal favorites because it really packs a punch, yet is quick and easy to make. It works very well with white fish too, if you prefer.**

**Serves 4–6**

- 1 tablespoon (15 ml) coconut oil
- 1 teaspoon cumin seeds
- 2 medium onions, blended in a food processor to a grated consistency
- 7 ounces (200 g) canned plum tomatoes
- 1 teaspoon salt
- 1 teaspoon turmeric
- ½ teaspoon chilli powder (optional)
- 2 to 3 green chillies, chopped
- approximately 1 cup (200 g) coconut cream
- 1 pound (500 g) chicken thighs, trimmed and cut into bite-size chunks
- 1 teaspoon garam masala
- handful of fresh coriander leaves, chopped

Heat the coconut oil in a pan until it melts and add the cumin seeds. When sizzling and aromatic, add the onions and fry until a golden color.

Add the tomatoes, salt, turmeric, chilli powder, and fresh chillies. Stir together and cook until the tomatoes break down, leaving a thick paste.

Pour in the coconut cream and cook gently for a few minutes so the flavors combine. Add the chicken, and stir to coat with the sauce.

Reduce the heat to the lowest setting, place the lid half on the pan, and cook for about 10 minutes.

Taste the sauce and adjust the seasoning if required.

Remove from the heat and add the garam masala, and sprinkle on the fresh coriander to serve.

# Malabari Prawns

This vibrant curry is all about South Indian coastal flavors, from the prawns to the coconut and curry leaves. The sauce is simply divine—the perfect balance of sweet, salt, bitter, and chilli. If you want to lighten it up, add kokum (a fruit used in South Indian cuisine as a souring agent), tamarind, or a squeeze of lime. I would recommend that you get the biggest, juiciest prawns you can find for this, but you can also use fish.

**Serves 4–6**

- 1 tablespoon (15 ml) coconut oil
- 1 teaspoon fenugreek seeds
- 5 garlic cloves, sliced
- 20 curry leaves
- 3-inch (7 cm) piece of fresh ginger, thinly sliced
- 2 to 3 green chillies, sliced diagonally
- 7 shallots, sliced
- 14 ounces (400 g) canned tomatoes
- 1 teaspoon salt
- 1 teaspoon turmeric
- 1 teaspoon hot red chilli powder
- 1 teaspoon coriander powder
- 3 tablespoons coconut powder
- approximately ¾ to 1 cup (200 ml) coconut milk
- 1 pound (500 g) king prawns, cleaned and deveined
- handful of fresh coriander leaves, chopped

Heat the oil in a pan over medium heat, add the fenugreek seeds, and stir for a few seconds (you don't want them to darken in color).

Add the sliced garlic and brown it before adding the curry leaves, sliced ginger, and sliced chillies. Stir and cook for 1 to 2 minutes.

Add the shallots and cook until soft and just starting to brown (about 10 minutes).

Using a hand blender or immersion blender, purée the canned tomatoes and add to the pan with the salt. Stir through and cook for a few minutes.

Add the turmeric, red chilli powder, and coriander powder and stir.

In a bowl, mix the coconut powder with some water to make a watery paste, and stir into the masala.

Bring to a boil, then reduce the heat to simmer until it's nice and thick. Add the coconut milk, and mix it together.

Once the sauce is thick and wonderfully rich in color at the desired consistency, check the seasoning and adjust if required. Stir in the raw prawns and cook until they change color.

Remove the pan from the heat, stir in the coriander leaves, and serve with some plain boiled rice.

# Tangy Tamarind Prawns

**Tamarind is a sour fruit native to India, used to add tang to dishes and chutneys. It's less harsh than lemon, and it enhances depth and color, too. I like to make this fairly spicy, so once I have dished up some for the kids, I add sliced fresh chillies just for me. The sauce is thick and rich, making it perfect to scoop up with poori or naan.**

**Serves 4–6**

- 2 tablespoons (30 ml) oil
- 1 teaspoon cumin seeds
- 1 onion, thinly sliced
- 2 garlic cloves, finely chopped
- 7 ounces (200 g) canned tomatoes
- 1 tablespoon fresh ginger, grated
- 1 teaspoon turmeric
- 1 teaspoon salt
- 1 chilli, finely chopped
- 1 tablespoon (15 g) tamarind paste (or a good squeeze of lemon juice)
- 1 pound (500 g) fresh king prawns, cleaned and deveined

**GARNISH**

- 2 fresh tomatoes, finely diced
- 1 teaspoon garam masala
- handful of fresh coriander leaves, chopped
- 2 chillies, sliced (optional)

Heat the oil in a pan over medium heat. Add the cumin seeds; when sizzling, add the onion and garlic. Fry gently until golden brown.

Once browned, reduce the heat and add the canned tomatoes, ginger, turmeric, salt, chilli, and tamarind paste. Increase the heat and stir so the tomatoes and onions melt together, creating a thick masala sauce.

Once the sauce is shiny, add the prawns and stir to coat them with the sauce. Reduce the heat and cook through for a few minutes.

Add the fresh tomatoes, stir and cook for a minute, and then remove from the heat.

Stir in the garam masala, sprinkle on the coriander, top with the chillies (optional), and serve.

# Vegetable Kofta Curry

Kofta, or meatless meatballs, can be made with any vegetables you have in the fridge. Chickpeas and cooked lentils work too. This recipe includes a creamy cashew nut sauce to put the kofta in, but you can also make them as a nibble or snack with a chutney or dip to dunk them into.

**Serves 4-6**

VEGETARIAN KOFTA

1 large potato

3 ounces (80 g) cauliflower florets

1½ ounces (40 g) green peas

1½ ounces (40 g) carrots

1½ ounces (40 g) green beans

1½ ounces (40 g) red pepper

1 green chilli

9 ounces (250 g) paneer

handful of fresh coriander leaves

1 teaspoon coriander seeds, crushed

1 teaspoon garam masala

1 teaspoon cumin seeds, crushed

1 teaspoon Kashmiri chilli powder

1 teaspoon mango powder

¼ teaspoon black pepper

1 teaspoon salt

¼ to ½ cup (25 to 50 g) gram flour

oil for frying

MASALA

2 tablespoons cashew nuts

1 onion

4 garlic cloves

3-inch (7 cm) piece of fresh ginger

1 green chilli

1 tablespoon rapeseed oil

1 teaspoon cumin seeds

1 bay leaf

4 green cardamom pods

3-inch (7 cm) piece of cassia bark

1 blade of mace

3 cloves

2 tomatoes or 7 ounces (200 g) canned tomatoes

1 teaspoon coriander seeds

½ teaspoon cumin seeds

1 teaspoon salt

1 teaspoon Kashmiri chilli powder

1 teaspoon turmeric

2 tablespoons (30 g) yogurt

1 teaspoon garam masala

VEGETABLE KOFTA

Add the vegetables—potato, cauliflower florets, green peas, carrots, beans, pepper, and green chilli—and the paneer into a food processor and blitz. Place the mixture into a bowl.

Chop the coriander leaves and add to the bowl along with the spices. Mix it all together.

Sprinkle in the gram flour a little at a time until it starts to bind the vegetables together.

Using one hand, squish everything together until it's thick and you can make balls with the mixture.

Heat the oil for frying the kofta. Test that it's hot enough by adding a little of the mixture—if it sinks, sizzles, and immediately floats back up, then it is ready. If it's too hot, the kofta will brown too quickly and remain raw inside.

Make golf ball–sized balls and very carefully place into the oil. Gently turn them to brown all over, about 3 to 5 minutes. Using a slotted spoon, remove to a dish lined with paper towels. Taste the first one to check that it's cooked inside and the seasoning is correct. If not, adjust the seasoning or return to the oil before cooking the rest. Cook the kofta in batches.

**MASALA**

Soak the cashews in hot water for around 20 minutes.

Place the onion, garlic, ginger, and chillies in a blender to make a smooth paste.

Heat the oil in a pan over medium heat and add the cumin seeds, bay leaf, green cardamom, cassia bark, mace, and cloves, and fry the spices until fragrant.

Add the onion paste and stir to cook until it starts to brown. If it catches, add a little splash of water and continue to cook. This will take about 20 minutes.

Grind the cashews with a little water to make a smooth paste and set aside.

Once the onions have browned, purée the tomatoes and add to the pan.

Grind the coriander and cumin seeds with a mortar and pestle. Add this and the salt, chilli powder, and turmeric and mix well. Cook until it starts to thicken, and then stir in the cashew paste.

Whip the yogurt with a little water to loosen it up. Stir in the yogurt and mix.

The sauce should be quite thick; add water to the pan to adjust the consistency so it's at a thickness you like.

Simmer for a few minutes, and then stir in the garam masala.

Add the kofta to the masala just before serving and cook for 2 minutes.

# Muttar Paneer

This is a real old-school Punjabi dish that plays an important part in the Indian diet, as many Indians are vegetarians. Paneer is also known as Indian cottage cheese. It is an acid-set cheese that is made from cow or buffalo milk. It's made by curdling milk with a fruit or vegetable acid, then pressing the curd until it's a solid block. It can be used as is, diced and fried, or grated and added to curries. The cheese is not aged; it doesn't melt; and it adds texture, much like tofu.

**Serves 4-6**

enough oil in a small pan to deep-fry the paneer

5 ounces (150 g) paneer, cut into approximately 2-inch (5 cm) cubes

1 tablespoon (15 ml) oil

1 teaspoon cumin seeds

1 onion, finely sliced

3 garlic cloves, sliced

9 ounces (250 g) canned plum tomatoes

1-inch (3 cm) piece of fresh ginger, grated

1 green chilli, finely chopped

1 teaspoon salt

1 teaspoon turmeric

1 teaspoon fenugreek powder (methi)

1 teaspoon Kashmiri chilli powder

7 ounces (200 g) frozen peas

1 teaspoon garam masala

handful of fresh coriander leaves, chopped

Heat enough oil in a pan to deep-fry the paneer over medium to high heat, and gently fry the paneer until golden brown. Remove and set on paper towels.

In another pan, heat more cooking oil and add the cumin seeds until they sizzle.

Add the onion and, after a few minutes, stir in the garlic. Cook for 10 minutes, until the onions are soft and turning golden.

When the onions are golden, add the tomatoes, ginger, chilli, salt, turmeric, fenugreek powder, and chilli powder. Using your stirring spoon, squish the tomatoes to break them down. Stir, and let the masala come together, about 10 minutes, until it becomes thick and shiny.

Once it's thick, add the fried paneer and frozen peas. Stir and cook for 2 to 3 minutes.

Pour in enough hot water to cover the paneer, and simmer for 10 minutes.

Remove from the heat, and sprinkle in the garam masala and fresh coriander to serve.

# Spiced Mushroom Pilau

**One-pot dishes are perfect for family dinners, and although this may look like a long list of ingredients, it's actually pretty simple to make. I know my kids aren't mushroom fans—apparently it's a texture thing—so you can substitute them for chicken or cauliflower if you prefer.**

**Serves 4-6**

7 ounces (200 g) basmati rice

**MUSHROOM MASALA**

2 to 3 tablespoons (30 to 45 ml) oil
1 teaspoon fennel seeds
1 teaspoon cumin seeds
1-inch (3 cm) piece of cassia bark
2 cloves
3 green cardamom pods
2 blades of mace
1 bay leaf
1 star anise
10 curry leaves
1 onion, finely chopped
6 garlic cloves, minced
3-inch (7 cm) piece of fresh ginger, minced
1 or 2 green chillies, finely chopped
1 tomato, finely chopped
1 teaspoon coriander powder
1 teaspoon turmeric powder
1 teaspoon red chilli powder
½ teaspoon garam masala powder
¼ teaspoon black pepper
1 teaspoon salt
9 ounces (250 g) chestnut mushrooms, cut into chunks
handful of fresh mint leaves, chopped
handful of fresh coriander leaves, chopped

Rinse the basmati rice in running water till the water runs clear of starch. Soak the rice in enough water to cover it and leave for 30 minutes. Then, drain the rice and set aside.

**MUSHROOM MASALA**

Heat the oil in a deep pan over medium heat, then add all the whole spices—fennel, cumin, cassia, cloves, green cardamom, mace, bay leaf, and star anise.

Stir in the curry leaves and fry the spices until fragrant for a few seconds, and then add chopped onions and sauté until they are translucent.

Add the minced garlic, minced ginger, and green chillies and cook until the garlic is lightly browned.

Add the chopped tomato and sauté for about 10 minutes.

Add the coriander powder, turmeric powder, red chilli powder, garam masala powder, black pepper, and salt.

Once fragrant and the tomatoes have broken down into the masala, add the mushrooms and half the mint and coriander leaves. Cook on low heat for 6 to 8 minutes.

Stir and add almost 1 cup (200 ml) of hot water. Bring the mixture to a simmer.

Add the rice and the remaining mint and coriander and stir through. Season with salt.

Reduce the heat and cover the pan with a lid. Cook for 10 minutes.

Once the water has been absorbed, check that the rice is cooked. If it still has a bite, add a little more water and cook with the lid on for a little longer.

Once the rice is cooked through, remove from the heat and let rest with the lid on for 5 minutes.

Remove the lid and fluff the rice before serving.

# Chana Masala with Spinach

**Chickpeas in a hearty tomato masala with the addition of spinach or kale makes a wonderful meat-free midweek meal that's quick and nutritious.**

**Serves 4-6**

- 1 to 2 tablespoons (15 to 30 ml) rapeseed oil
- ½ teaspoon mustard seeds
- 1 teaspoon cumin seeds
- 1 large onion, diced
- 4 garlic cloves, crushed
- 4 plum tomatoes or 7 ounces (200 g) canned tomatoes
- 1 heaped teaspoon coriander seeds, crushed
- 1 green chilli, chopped
- 1 teaspoon red chilli powder
- 1 teaspoon turmeric
- 1 teaspoon salt, or to taste
- 28 ounces (800 g) (2 14-ounce cans) chickpeas, drained and rinsed
- 7 ounces (200 g) spinach or kale, roughly chopped
- 1 green chilli, sliced for garnish

Heat the oil in a lidded pan over medium heat, and add the mustard and cumin seeds.

Stir for a minute until you can smell the aroma of the mustard and cumin seeds; when they stop sizzling, add the diced onions.

Fry the onions for 15 minutes until they start to brown, then add the garlic. Fry together for 4 minutes before adding the tomatoes. Stir and cook for a few minutes. Add a little water if required.

Add the crushed coriander, green chilli, chilli powder, turmeric, and salt. Cook on a gentle heat until the tomatoes start to break down and create a thick masala sauce (about 10 minutes).

Turn the heat up to thicken the sauce a little if required. Add the chickpeas and stir to coat them with the masala. Add a splash of water and let them simmer for 5 minutes.

Add the chopped spinach, a handful at a time, stirring in between. Remove from the heat and allow the spinach to wilt through the dish.

Top with the sliced chilli and serve with poori and fresh plain yogurt.

**Top Tip • If your kids are a bit anti-veg, remove their portion before adding the spinach to the dish. They will love scooping this up with the poori.**

# Pineapple Curry

**I know what you're thinking—it's a weird one! But I personally love this South Indian specialty. Coastal flavors, creamy coconut, hot chillies, zingy pineapple—what's not to love? Plus, it cooks down to a wonderful meaty texture, yet it's totally vegan!**

**Serves 4–6**

- 1 tablespoon (15 ml) coconut oil
- 1 teaspoon mustard seeds
- 4 cardamom pods
- ¾-inch (2 cm) piece of cassia bark
- 1 onion, diced
- 4 garlic cloves, minced
- 1-inch (3 cm) piece of fresh ginger, grated
- 1 red chilli, sliced
- 1 teaspoon turmeric
- 1 teaspoon lemon pepper, crushed (or just black pepper)
- ½ teaspoon chilli powder
- ½ teaspoon salt, or to taste
- 1 pineapple, peeled, cored, and diced
- 1¾ cups (400 ml) coconut milk

Heat the coconut oil in a pan over medium heat and add the mustard seeds, cardamom, and cassia bark until the seeds pop.

Add the diced onion and stir until translucent.

Add the garlic and cook for about 5 minutes.

As the onions just start to brown, add the ginger, chilli, turmeric, pepper, chilli powder, and salt, and stir.

Add the pineapple pieces and coat with the masala spices.

Pour in the coconut milk and turn up the heat to bring to a simmer.

Put the lid on and simmer gently for 30 minutes or until you are happy with how much the pineapple has softened—I prefer mine soft.

# 4

# Simple Sides

Sides are an important part of the Indian meal, and while I like to call them simple (because they mostly are), they can actually make or break a great meal. Many prefer to go for a low-carb side dish such as a cauliflower rice, but whether it's plain rice, breads, pulses, rotis, or couscous, there is always a great dish on the side to carry the meal to a heavenly place.

# Basic Fluffy Basmati Rice

**Serves 4-6**

2 cups (390 g) basmati rice
4 cups (960 ml) cold water

Wash the rice until the water runs clear. Do this by putting the rice in a pan, covering with warm water, and gently stirring with your hand. Drain and wash again until the water is clear. You will need to do this about four times. I always measure my rice in a mug (a standard mug will feed three to four people) and you will need twice the amount of water by volume to rice to cook it perfectly.

Put your washed rice in a wide-based pan and add twice the amount of cold water. Heat up the pan and bring it to a rolling boil (until it's steaming). Reduce the heat to the lowest setting possible and put the lid on the pan. Cook for exactly 10 minutes. However tempted you may be, do not remove the lid before then. After 10 minutes, remove from the heat, and let it sit for a minute. Then take the lid off and let the steam rise.

All the water will have been absorbed and each grain will be separate and standing on end. Using a fork, gently fluff up the rice; don't just plunge straight in with a spoon.

To salt or not to salt—here's my answer: Adding salt does enhance its flavor, but if you are cooking rice to have as a side to a flavorful curry, salt is not needed. When rice is the main ingredient, then yes, you should season it.

## PLAIN RICE

Cooking rice seems to be somewhat of a dark art for most, and it's the one thing I get asked about the most often. Here are my rice rules:

- Always buy the best rice you can.
- Choose basmati rice for Indian food.
- Be gentle, so you don't break the grains.
- Always wash your rice.
- When your rice is cooking, however tempted you may be, just leave it alone, don't take the lid off, don't stir it, and don't mess with it!

# Zaffrani Pilau

**A dish I learned to cook in my restaurant days, this is one for a decadent evening—a little unusual but worth the effort if you are looking to impress. Fragranced with cumin and saffron, the rice is cooked in cream and then baked—it doesn't get any better than that!**

**Serves 4-6**

- 1⅓ cups (260 g) basmati rice
- 1 tablespoon (15 ml) vegetable oil
- 1 teaspoon cumin seeds
- 1 teaspoon salt
- 1 teaspoon butter
- 3 to 4 tablespoons (50 ml) cream
- strand of saffron

Wash the rice in two or three changes of water until the starch water runs clear. Then soak in warm water for 30 minutes. Preheat the oven to 350°F (180°C, or gas mark 4).

Boil 1¼ cups (300 ml) water in a kettle and set aside.

In a wide-based pan, add the oil and place over medium heat before adding the cumin seeds.

Fry for 30 seconds until you can smell the cumin aroma, and pour in the boiling water, salt, butter, and cream.

Bring the water to a boil, drain the rice, and add it to the pan. Bring back to a boil. Cook until the water has just been absorbed (about 6 minutes).

Remove from the heat and wet a clean tea towel. Cover the rice first with the wet tea towel and then with the lid of the pan.

Place the pan in the oven for 8 minutes.

Meanwhile, crush the saffron strand with a mortar and pestle and add a little warm water. Allow it to steep.

Remove the pan from the oven, and remove the lid and the tea towel (be careful—it will be hot). Check that the rice is cooked, and then let the rice stand for a few minutes. If it's not cooked, leave in the oven for another couple of minutes.

Pour in streaks of the saffron water and very gently fork through the rice before serving.

# Lemon Rice

**Rice is so versatile that you can let your creativity run wild. I call this sunshine in a bowl because it's a beautiful vibrant yellow rice that's fragranced with South Indian flavors. Not only is it beautiful to look at, but it has textures that will impress everyone. Great in the summer as a barbecue side dish or with grilled chicken or fish.**

**Serves 4-6**

1 cup (200 g) basmati rice
2 tablespoons (30 ml) coconut oil
1 teaspoon mustard seeds
1 tablespoon unsalted peanuts
1 tablespoon unsalted cashew nuts
7 to 10 curry leaves
1 teaspoon salt
½ teaspoon turmeric powder
2 lemons, cut in halves

Cook the rice using the Basic Fluffy Basmati Rice recipe on page 88. Once the rice is cooked, remove to a tray to cool.

In a wide pan or wok, heat the coconut oil over medium heat and add the mustard seeds. As they begin to sputter, add the peanuts first. After a couple of minutes, add the cashews, and fry to a golden brown color. (Don't let the nuts burn.)

Working very quickly, add the curry leaves, salt, and turmeric powder, and fry for a minute. Remove from the heat and stir in the cooled rice.

Squeeze in the juice from the lemon and carefully mix through until all the rice is beautifully bright yellow.

**Top Tip • The nuts will burn very quickly, so before you start cooking, have everything ready to go. If the nuts burn, you will need to start again, unless you like a bitter flavor.**

# Roti/Phulka

**I love roti and have been known to eat a fair few in one sitting. An absolute staple of North Indian food, these are made from atta, which is a whole wheat flour that comes from hard wheat grown across the Indian subcontinent. This light, creamy brown flour is made by grinding the whole of the wheat grain. Because atta has a high gluten content, the dough can be rolled out nice and thin and toasted on a griddle pan until it puffs up like a little pillow of air. There is a real skill to making roti—I have been making these since I was nine years old, and even now my mother complains that they are not thin and round enough! If you can't find atta, substitute equal amounts of whole wheat flour and plain flour.**

**Makes 10–12**

4¼ cups (500 g) whole wheat flour (atta)

approximately 1¼ cups (300 ml) water

1 teaspoon butter or oil

**Top Tip • A tawa is an Indian griddle pan used to make breads; it's a thin cast-iron skillet. If you don't have one, just use a frying pan.**

Put the atta in a bowl and, adding a little water at a time, use your fingers to bring the flour together to make the dough.

Knead the dough using your knuckles, folding it over as you go. The dough should come together and come away from your hand and the bowl. If it is sticky, add a little more flour and continue to knead. The dough needs to be soft but not sloppy. Place the dough into a container with a lid so it doesn't dry out, and set aside for at least 30 minutes before making the roti.

Put some dry atta on a flat plate for dusting. Heat up the tawa (Indian griddle pan) or nonstick frying pan on the lowest setting, flour your hands, and take a tangerine-sized ball of dough.

Roll the dough in the palms of your hands, creating a smooth ball.

Flatten it out, flour the disc again, and roll it out. Turn it over, and flour and roll again, trying not to let it stick. When it is about 3 inches (7 cm) in diameter, pick it up and pass from one hand to the other as if you are clapping. This evens it out and removes the excess dry flour.

On the heated tawa, carefully place the flattened roti. Try not to let the roti fold. You will see the color of the roti darken after about 10 seconds; turn the roti over and increase the heat when bubbles appear after about 10 seconds, take the tawa off the hob, and put the roti directly onto the flame.

The roti will begin to puff up; turn it over using tongs and move it around so it doesn't burn. If you are not using a gas range or are not comfortable using a naked flame, leave the roti on the pan. Turn the heat down a little and when bubbles appear, turn the roti over. Using a clean tea towel, gently press the top of the roti, which will begin to blow up with hot steam.

Work quickly, turning and pressing until it has all puffed up. Be careful not to burn yourself. Remove the roti, set it on a clean tea towel, and cover to keep warm.

# Naan—Plain/Blue Cheese/Garlic/ Truffle

Traditionally, naan dough is naturally leavened with live yogurt, which aerates it and makes the bread light and fluffy. It's then hand-stretched and slapped onto the inside wall of a tandoor oven where it bakes and becomes crisp on one side and bubbly and soft on the other. This cooking method gives it a unique texture and smokiness. When my mum first came to the United Kingdom, she used all sorts of crazy things to get those precious little bubbles into the naan dough, from lemonade to original Andrews Salts (yes, the tummy antacid). I now have a formula to make the naan light and airy that will work at home in your kitchen. I have also given you a couple of different cooking methods to try—you will never buy naan again.

**Makes 4**

- 1 teaspoon dried active yeast
- 1 teaspoon sugar
- 1⅔ cups (200 g) plain flour
- 1 teaspoon black onion seeds (or a handful of chopped coriander leaves)
- ½ teaspoon salt
- ½ teaspoon baking powder
- 1 tablespoon (15 ml) vegetable oil
- 2 tablespoons (30 g) plain yogurt
- 2 tablespoons (30 ml) milk

**Top Tips**

- **To make blue cheese naan, add 4 tablespoons (28 g) blue cheese into the dough.**
- **To make garlic naan, heat 2 tablespoons (30 ml) ghee and add 2 cloves crushed garlic until soft. Smear over the cooked naan.**
- **To make truffle naan, smear ghee over the cooked naan and sprinkle with truffle shavings.**

In a small bowl, mix the yeast and sugar with a tablespoon of warm water to activate. Let sit for 5 minutes in a warm place until frothy.

In a separate bowl mix the flour, onion seeds, salt, and baking powder. When the yeast is frothy, add it to the flour with the oil and yogurt.

Knead the dough with slightly wet hands, folding as you go. If it feels a little dry, add some milk and continue to knead. Once it's nice and soft, cover the bowl with a damp tea towel and leave it in a warm place to rise for at least 1 hour (but longer if possible).

Divide the dough into four balls and place on a floured surface. Roll each ball out until it's about ¼ inch (6 mm) thick.

### GRILL METHOD

Turn the grill on to high. Heat a tawa (flat Indian griddle pan) or a frying pan and lace the naan onto it for a couple of seconds to brown on one side.

Transfer to a baking tray (seared side down) and place in the hot grill for 2 to 5 minutes, and watch the magic as they puff up.

### TAWA METHOD

Sprinkle one side of the naan dough with water. Place the wet side of the naan on a hot tawa (Indian griddle pan). Once the bread starts to bubble, turn the pan with the half-cooked naan on it upside down over the flames on your stove so the top of the naan starts to char and bubble and cooks all the way through. This is a great way to replicate a tandoor.

Smear the naan with butter and enjoy.

# Turmeric & Honey Bread

Making bread interesting with the use of spices is so much fun, allowing you to get creative and try new things. This recipe was created to dunk into a heart-warming soup. Once you start baking your own bread, it's hard to go back to the store-bought stuff. I have used atta here, but you can use a strong bread flour as well.

**Serves 4-6**

1¾ teaspoons (7 g) yeast
5 tablespoons (75 ml) warm water
½ teaspoon sugar
3⅓ cups (400 g) atta
2 tablespoons (30 g) yogurt
2 tablespoons (30 ml) ghee
2 tablespoons (30 g) honey
1 teaspoon salt
2 teaspoons kalonji seeds
2 teaspoons turmeric
approximately ¾ cup (150 to 200 ml) water

In a small bowl, combine the yeast, warm water, and sugar, and stir. Let sit for 5 to 10 minutes until frothy.

Place all the other ingredients into a bowl except the water.

Pour in the yeast and slowly add the water a little at a time. The amount of water needed can vary depending on the flour, so be careful.

Knead the dough until it comes together and is soft. Or you can use a mixer with a dough hook to do the same job.

Place the dough in an oiled bowl and cover for 1 hour with a clean, wet tea towel. Leave it in a warm place for it to rise.

Once it has doubled in size, knock it back and knead for a minute or so.

Oil a baking tray, shape the dough into a dome shape, and place on the tray.

Cover again with the tea towel and leave for another hour in a warm place.

Preheat the oven to 400°F (200°C, or gas mark 6) and, once the dough has again doubled in size, bake in the oven for 20 to 25 minutes.

Once it turns a golden color, remove from the oven. When you tap the bottom, it should sound hollow. Leave it on a cooling rack until completely cooled.

**Top Tip • If you find you have made the dough too wet, just add more dry flour until you have a nice, soft dough.**

# Chilla Pancakes

**These little green Indian pancakes are a great side bread if you are gluten intolerant, or they make a light, healthy breakfast. They are made with mung beans, which are a light, healthy lentil used for so many different dishes. Light and easy to digest, they taste fantastic. The lentils need to be soaked so they are soft before being blitzed to make a batter, so ensure you give yourself plenty of time to prepare.**

**Makes 8-10**

- 3½ ounces (100 g) moong dhal (mung beans), whole or split with husk
- ½ small onion, chopped
- 1 teaspoon fresh ginger, grated
- 1 teaspoon fresh coriander leaves, chopped
- salt to taste
- 1 green chilli, chopped
- 2 to 3 tablespoons (30 to 45 ml) water
- 1 ounce (30 g) green peas or a handful of spinach (optional)
- 1 teaspoon baking soda
- 1 tablespoon (15 ml) ghee or oil, to cook

Soak the moong dhal (mung beans) for 4 hours in a cup of water.

Blitz in a blender with the onion, ginger, coriander, salt, and chilli. Add a little more water to make a thick paste. If using green peas or spinach, blanch in hot water, drain, and add to the blender.

Only when you are ready to cook, add the baking soda and mix everything together. It should be the consistency of thick pancake batter. Add more water if required.

Heat a frying pan or a small egg frying pan to high, then reduce the heat. Add a teaspoon of ghee or oil to coat the pan. Pour in a ladle full of the batter and spread around the pan with the back of a spoon.

Cook for a few minutes. When the top is dry, drizzle on a little more oil and flip it over to cook the other side. They are very delicate, so cook gently (4 to 5 minutes).

Repeat with the remaining mixture and serve hot. They turn quite dark in color, so don't be too surprised!

# Spruced-Up Cauliflower Rice

Rice is the basic staple when it comes to Indian food, but if you prefer something less carb heavy, there are other options: brown rice, couscous, polenta, or this lovely cauliflower rice. Much lighter than rice as a side, it becomes a dish in its own right by infusing loads of aromatics into it. This also works as a superb meal to take to work in your lunch box.

**Serves 4**

1 medium cauliflower
1 tablespoon (15 ml) rapeseed oil
1 teaspoon black mustard seeds
1 teaspoon cumin seeds
2 dried Kashmiri chillies, each broken into 3 or 4 pieces
1 garlic clove, sliced
2-inch (5 cm) piece of fresh ginger, finely grated
½ teaspoon turmeric
1 teaspoon salt
2 fresh green chillies, sliced

Roughly chop your cauliflower, put into a blender, and blitz very quickly to get a fine shred of cauliflower.

Heat the oil on medium heat in a large saucepan or karahi. When it is hot, add the mustard seeds, followed by the cumin seeds and dried chillies.

Stir for about 30 seconds, and then add the sliced garlic, grated ginger, turmeric, and salt. Fry for 30 seconds.

Stir in the cauliflower rice and stir-fry for about 3 to 4 minutes over medium heat. Stir in the green chillies.